Great English Churchmen Series

# JOHN WESLEY

MACMILLAN AND CO., Limited
LONDON · BOMBAY · CALCUTTA · MADRAS
MELBOURNE

THE MACMILLAN COMPANY
NEW YORK · BOSTON · CHICAGO
DALLAS · SAN FRANCISCO

THE MACMILLAN CO. OF CANADA, Ltd.
TORONTO

# JOHN WESLEY

BY

## WILLIAM HOLDEN HUTTON, D.D.

DEAN OF WINCHESTER

HONORARY FELLOW OF S. JOHN'S COLLEGE, OXFORD
A CHAPLAIN OF THE ORDER OF S. JOHN OF JERUSALEM
HON. D.C.L. DURHAM

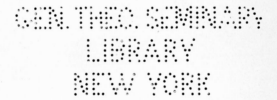

MACMILLAN AND CO., LIMITED
ST. MARTIN'S STREET, LONDON

1927

COPYRIGHT

PRINTED IN GREAT BRITAIN
BY R. & R. CLARK, LIMITED, EDINBURGH

# GENERAL PREFACE

THE intention of this series of studies of the lives of English bishops and priests is to suggest the significance of the man in the age in which he lived and in the movements within the Church with which he was concerned. It is the general editorial policy to select a biographer sympathetic with the character with whom he deals, since, in the view of the editor, sympathy is necessary to understanding. The choice of subjects is entirely arbitrary, following no chronological order and no settled plan, and the writers represent every school of thought in the English Church. Each volume is individual, and the writer alone is responsible for its judgements.

# PREFACE

THOUGH there have been among English religious leaders some who were certainly wiser, and perhaps better, men, there has never been one who made so great a mark upon the history of the country, and, it may be, even more, beyond its shores as did John Wesley. Anselm was a much greater man, Joseph Butler a much wiser, Matthew Parker was much more prudent, much more statesmanlike, there was more of the pure saint in Edward Pusey and John Keble and Richard Meux Benson ; but none of them, it is safe to say, moved more men and women to a life of holiness and philanthropy.

To the great religious movement of which he was the leader, Lecky attributes the fact that the doctrines of the French Revolution never took root in England. He is quite right. The sentimentalism (a word Wesley

hated) of the French reformers was diverted
by his preaching, and by his disciples, into
another channel ; and, if its issue in practical
philanthropy was delayed, it eventually became more intense and more secure. The
influence of his teaching also emerged as the
defeat of Calvinism. The history of England
proves the success of the swashing blows
which Wesley dealt against Calvinism and
on behalf of spiritual and moral emancipation.

That quaint but genuine preacher, Bishop
Thorold of Winchester, once said, " It is very
easy to throw stones at Jacob : *and they hit* ".
That is equally true of Wesley. Horace
Walpole said he was

as evidently an actor as Garrick. He spoke his
sermon, but so fast, and with so little accent, that
I am sure he has often uttered it, for it was like a
lesson. There were parts and eloquence in it ;
but towards the end he exalted his voice and acted
very ugly enthusiasm : decried learning, and told
stories, like Latimer, of the fool of his college,
who said " I thanks God for everything ".

The meaning of which certainly is that he
was a popular preacher of the highest class.
In his own time, and since, people have made
merry over his love affairs, and derided him

because his wife dragged him across the floor by his hair. But no one now doubts the purity of his life or the simplicity of his heart. He could use the most violent language to others when he reproached them for their own: he said that of one of his own preachers was " such as an archangel would not use to the devil ". But also he could be a very angel of gentleness ; and men and women all over the three kingdoms loved him for it.

Unlike so many of the " revivalists " of the century before him, Wesley believed with all his heart in a corporate religion. " I am no friend to solitary Christianity," he said ; and the greatest work of his life was to build up an organisation which should help ordinary folk to serve God and man in a close companionship of love. That this led to a larger disunion of English Christians was quite contrary to his emphatic and repeated wish ; yet his impetuosity and self-will, quite as much as a jealous and timid conservatism among Church leaders—*episcopi Anglicani semper pavidi*—were to blame for it. Autocratic, overbearing, imbued to a quite astounding degree with a belief in his own capacity to advise every human being on every conceivable subject, a child, a pretty girl, a scholar, a country clergyman, a soldier, an old woman, and a prime minister, yet he was an eminently lovable man because so full of the milk of human kindness and so absolutely sincere.   He was often taken in, as good men always are ; but when he could give himself to know a man—not always, it must be admitted, a woman,—he could give sound, indeed quite admirable advice.

The year 1926 is one in which most fitly a humble tribute to his memory may be paid. It marks the two hundredth anniversary of his connection with one of the two colleges in Oxford with which his memory will always be associated.

The bi-centenary of his election as a Fellow of Lincoln on March 17, 1726, was commemorated this year by a dinner at the college, a service in the college chapel, and a breakfast in the hall of Christ Church. Representatives of the various Methodist bodies were present at these gatherings.

This will have been a new beginning of pilgrimages to the Oxford home of the great man.

Those who visit the colleges where, in the language of the time, he was bred, will look upon three interesting portraits—two at Lincoln College, one at Christ Church. Those at Lincoln show him in youth and in old age ; that at Christ Church, charming, gracious, smiling, best expresses the beauty which those who loved him saw as they looked through the face to the soul within. More beautiful still are the pictures of him in extreme old age—such as Hamilton's, in the National Portrait Gallery—which show a strange, wistful air of happy expectation, such as illumined the faces of John Keble and Edward King. His sermons, when they are read, no more explain, than do Mr. Gladstone's speeches, the influence of the man. His letters, simple, sometimes humorous, always direct, written with unresting pen, show what he was. And the overwhelming evidence of contemporaries establishes him as " a man of great views, great energy, and great virtues ".

With Oxford his name, like these of other great religious leaders, will always be associated : and so will the country of his birth.

He was, in some ways, a typical Lincolnshire man, conscientious, sturdy, sensitive, and independent. All those qualities he showed as a college tutor, a Christian minister working in Oxford among the poor, and as the founder of a little society which should actively carry out the principles of the Church. He was almost a typical Oxford man—a student of the classics and of the literature of his day, a very neat, well-dressed person, a highly emotional person, a very determined and obstinate person, keen and heart-set upon the practical issues of life. While Bacon, the Cambridge man, took all knowledge for his province, Wesley, of Oxford, took the whole world for his parish.

There are many who will echo the last words of Southey's Life as they think of that reunion among Christians which the commemoration may well prefigure :

The obstacles to this are surely not insuperable, perhaps not so difficult as they may appear. And, were this effected, John Wesley would then be ranked, not only among the most remarkable and influential men of his age, but among the great benefactors of his country and his kind.

A student of John Wesley to-day has many advantages : the literature surrounding his life is enormous. Of no religious leader of modern times, I think, is there such a cult, and many able and sincere writers ever since his death have eulogised him, short of idolatry. I will not attempt a bibliography. I will merely say here which are the materials on which I myself have chiefly relied in my attempt to reconstruct his life and estimate his work. First, of course, stand his own writings, and chiefest by far the wonderful *Journal*, almost the most remarkable auto-biography ever written. The edition of Dr. Nehemiah Curnock (8 vols., Epworth Press) is a splendid monument of piety. Then, among the Lives, stand out Southey's really delightful biography (admirably edited, 1925, by the Rev. Maurice FitzGerald), and Tyerman's *Life and Times* (1880). Dr. Overton's sketch is full of sympathy and understanding, as befits a Rector of Epworth. *The New History of Methodism*, published in 1909, is very useful. A very valuable monograph is that of Professor Leger (*John Wesley's Last Love*, 1910). The most recent and com-

prehensive studies are those by Dr. John
Simon.  Happily his work is not yet complete, but he has already dealt with Wesley
in his relation to *The Religious Societies* (a
valuable addition to our knowledge), *The
Methodist Societies*, and *The Advance of
Methodism*, bringing the history down to
1756. Mr. Eayrs has made an excellent
selection of the letters.  Among general
histories the information, and the estimates,
contained in the works of Lecky and Abbey
and Overton, are of great use to the student
who desires to see Wesley and his age from
every point of view.  To these, and many
more books, any biographer of Wesley must
be indebted.  But most of all must any who
write of John Wesley feel indebted to himself and grateful for the privilege of describ-
ing, inadequately as it must needs be, something of the worth and character of a great
and good man.

Some pages in this book have previously
appeared in print.  For permission to use
them now I have to thank the *Times* and the
*Guardian*.

For much help, especially in the correction

of proofs, I am greatly indebted to Mrs.
W. H. Savile, whose kindness to me has
been unfailingly given for the sake of her
husband, who was my constant friend for
forty-five years.

W. H. HUTTON.

THE DEANERY, WINCHESTER,
    *Michaelmas* 1926.

# CONTENTS

# CHAPTER I

## THE EARLY YEARS

It was a habit of the nineteenth century, at least in its later years, to condemn or to scoff at the eighteenth. It was too cold-hearted and hot-blooded. It ate and drank too much and prayed too little. It did not understand Art or appreciate Nature. It was too bucolic, too bellicose, too dilettante, too dull. If it went into the country it either thrust good men like Parson Adams into pig-styes, or it dressed up blowsy milkmaids like porcelain shepherdesses. It knew nothing of the Romantic literature or the Tractarian theology. All these charges are serious, and some of them are true. But the twentieth century has begun to regard the nineteenth as ignorant and hypocritical; and though it would probably be horrified in fact at the eighteenth, it has, in fancy, begun to believe it not so black as it was painted. Yet no century has less affinity with common sense than the twentieth ; and the eighteenth is *par excellence* the age of common sense. It may be difficult then to-day rightly to appraise that period : but the attempt is worth making, and now it is made by one who has more of the nineteenth than the twentieth in his experience.

Historians of each century in past history have taken pleasure in finding for each its typical characters and its greatest men. The task is not an easy one, and certainly it has not always been successfully attempted. The difficulty is increased, of course, by the fact that lives will not be confined to one century, and great men have a tendency to be prophetic in their influence. Yet typical men are not hard to discover, and sometimes their greatness is beyond question. Justinian of the sixth century, Muhammad of the seventh cannot be disputed : nor can Charles the Great of the ninth, Gregory VII. of the eleventh, S. Bernard of the twelfth, Edward I. and S. Louis and S. Francis, not alone in the thirteenth—a veritable age of great men. Then difficulties arise, and persistent national jealousies appear. We shall hardly agree about the fourteenth or fifteenth centuries, and for the sixteenth Ignatius of Loyola may perhaps be Luther's rival. For the seventeenth Louis XIV. seems at last to be coming into his own, though Peter the Great cannot be obliterated so easily as the name of the city he founded. We need not attempt the nineteenth century : it has puzzles of its own : some would put Bismarck and even Mazzini and Darwin beside Napoleon Buonaparte. But of the eighteenth the hero, or the type, has been hard to find. Pitt, Frederick II., Voltaire, George Washington, have their champions ; but there is at least a very considerable body of quite independent and unprejudiced opinion which would pronounce in favour of John Wesley. His characteristics, in narrowness as well as in breadth, are certainly those of his own age, raised again and again to a higher power : of the best side of the eighteenth century he is certainly typical. He was indeed an Organiser of Victory, and, one might say, the first of the Benevolent Despots. And when it comes to the nice calculation of greatness by its influence on mankind what can discount the fame of one who transformed the religion of a race, which is spreading—and his influence with it—over the whole world ? Wesley's influence is as wide and as enduring as Napoleon's, and more permanent than Bismarck's. A typical writer of Victorian England said that " the pen is mightier than the sword ", and with Wesley the influence of the voice, precarious and ephemeral as it seems, was added to the indomitable force of the character. He spoke, and believed his words were literature and life. This does not mean that Europe will ever think Wesley so great a man as Napoleon, or Englishmen justly admire him so much as the younger Pitt. But it means that his greatness is incontestable and his influence still unimpaired.

Now that a century has passed since his birth, it is time to see from a survey of his life, his writings, and his character, how this man —in the eyes of the twentieth century obscurely born and imperfectly educated—rose to be the leader of what was almost a religious revolution—though revolutionary is nearly the last word to apply to his character or his opinions—and an inspirer of millions in his own country and his own age, and, beyond both, across the ages and over the habitable globe.

John Wesley was born on June 17, 1703, at Epworth Rectory, in the Isle of Axholme, at the north-west of Lincolnshire. The formative influences of his youth were two persons and two events : his father and mother, the rectory fire, and the rectory ghost. Looking behind these to his ancestry we find a certain hereditary strength or determination or conscientious obstinacy, a desire to run rather against than with the current. The critical might say that he had non-conformity in his blood. Dr. Annesley, once rector of S. Giles's, Cripplegate, and then minister of a meeting-house in Little S. Helen's, was a pertinacious dissident, of whose physical strength—which his grandson inherited—Antony Wood records that " he seldom drank any beer, only water, nevertheless he was rarely sick, and his sight was so strong he could read the smallest print in his seventy-seventh year ".

In the career of the Wesleys, the family influences, the Westleys and Annesleys, supply many significant points. Dissenting ancestry helps us to answer how it was that the child of two such determined Churchfolk as the Rector of Epworth and his wife, while stoutly, and even defiantly, professing to the end to remain a member of the National Church, should yet be the parent of a body which felt itself compelled to dissent.

No history of the brothers John and Charles, nor any study of the movement in which they were the chief forces, can be complete or convincing which ignores the influence of their remarkable parents. And as is so often the case with good men, and great men too, the mother comes first. Susanna Annesley married (? in 1690) Samuel Wesley, also originally of dissenting opinions, but after his sojourn at the University a staunch and deliberate Churchman. They had nineteen children, of whom John was the fifteenth. The father was a very strict, very conscientious and sensible, but rather narrow man. The mother was a woman of very great strength and beauty of character, and certainly she had, like the lady whom Dr. Johnson mentioned, a " bottom of good sense ". Perhaps the best epithet to apply to her is " serene ". When she accepted the membership of the Church she became a devoted Churchwoman, fortified by her favourite George Herbert, by Jeremy Taylor, Ken, Pascal, and the *Imitation of Christ*. Vigorous in mind as in body, she was a most wise as well as an affectionate mother, and to her children, as John said, a true " preacher of righteousness ". All through the formative years of her son's life she was his wise and loving adviser. She died when he was on the verge of forty. It might be possible to trace in him after that date a less well - regulated mind. Samuel

Wesley, the father, was, in no disparaging sense of the words, ascetic and fanatical : a highly determined person in politics and religion. He was decidedly, in the language of the times, a High Churchman. When he accepted the doctrines of the Church of England he saw that it involved an acceptance of the decisions of the Church Universal : thus many opinions which modern questioners have decided to call obscurantist, romanising, or extreme, were to him the necessary and natural fundamentals of Catholic belief. A proctor of the clergy in the diocese of Lincoln, he was now and then in London, yet for the greater part of his life he was a simple, yet learned, country parson, suffering like so many of his tribe, from dire poverty unflinchingly borne, and buoyed up by the delights of continual study and occasional publication. It was a recreation, as it has been to so many country clergy, to write a rather odd book or two. He was certainly odd himself, as the eccentric headdress in the portraits of him shows. But he was a very candid, simple-minded, strenuous person : the worthy father of so illustrious a son, whom he and his wife undoubtedly inspired yet never overshadowed.

Of the events, the fire in 1709, from which John was with difficulty rescued, made more impression on the mother than the son : she saw that he was destined for the fall and rising again of many in Israel. The ghost (1716–17), if such it was, which survived a closer scrutiny than the lady of Cock-lane, was a *polter-geist* : no one was a penny the worse for its pranks. Yet John, it is quite safe to conclude, was then indoctrined with a strong tendency to superstition, or at least credulity ; he always maintained the super-natural nature of the phenomena.

Unkind critics would say that John Wesley was brought up in an atmosphere of as-ceticism and superstition : there are traces of each in his later life ; but strong parental common sense triumphed. He was all through his life an extremely practical per-sonage. And to be practical is generally considered to be a special characteristic of North - country Englishmen. Lincolnshire may geographically belong to the Midlands, and ethnologically there may be a good many descendants of Mercian Saxons in the county, but there are quite as many of Danish blood, and its speech retains a great deal of affinity with that of those who live north of the Humber. A Yorkshire man can make nothing of the talk of a Hampshire man, and a Lincolnshire man is often almost as much puzzled by it. But Lincoln can understand York and Durham, and canny Newcastle can understand the men of Lindsey. Wesley's birthplace and his early life fitted him to understand the North, and his Oxford training brought him to know the South. If he learnt to understand south-erners and to adopt some of their manners, their speech, and their way of thinking, he really belonged all his life to the North, to that land of wide spaces and open vision, of strange imaginings and fundamental sin-cerities which, among the dwellers in country villages especially, belong to the men of Lincolnshire. Not so shrewd, or perhaps so selfish, as Yorkshire men, they are almost as direct, quite as candid, as keenly observant of the facts of life, as open—so certain of their own poets have shown—to the spiritual influences of nature and religion, and as wake-ful for the call of God and man. And over all the northern parts of the shire, betwixt sea and wold and Trent and Humber, there still clings a strange sense of isolation, of the loneliness in which men are often bred to stand up against the storms of life.

The Isle of Axholme, which still retains many of its ancient characteristics, its loneli-ness, its treeless distances, its carefully kept dykes—dyke in its Northern meaning, " a channel to receive water ", says Dr. Johnson, referring to Pope—its windmills, its rare birds, its bleak winds, was in Wesley's time much more nearly a real island. Like the Isle of Ely, it was fenland emerging as it were from the water, and its population had the independence and roughness of an amphibious race. There were no monks singing evensong, as Cnut heard at Ely. The revival of religion, none the less, was to begin there : on new lines, it may be, which yet at first did not perceptibly diverge from the old.

To the two parishes where his father ministered belong the earliest influences of John Wesley's life ; and there he returned after his Oxford training to recover, as it were, the touch of common life. Has " the isle ", as men around call it, much altered in the last two hundred years ? Epworth is still to-day a large and flourishing village, with claims perhaps to be a town, for its population is given as 1853. The fine rectory stands in ample grounds surrounded by high walls over which its high trees rise conspicuous in a land where trees are few. The solitary fertility of the Isle of Axholme, " flat as a pancake ", the absence of trees

and houses and barns, the presence of windmills, the wide dykes through which the
sluggish waters flow, the long straight roads,
give to the country a Hollandish air. " Ca-
naille, canards, canaux ", in the days before
he was well known and loved for what he
was, perhaps Wesley may have been tempted
to say, borrowing for once from the Voltaire
whom he reprobated. The benefice appears
now to be not nearly so valuable as it was
years ago, and Wesleyanism has, naturally,
established a firm hold among the people.
Yet still the parish church retains the dignity
of old, its fifteenth-century solidity surviving,
but its ancient spaciousness dwarfed by the
wooden partition, painted to look like stone,
and with a quaint " Gothic " window therein,
which screens off the western end and makes
of it a belfry and vestries. It stands high
above the surrounding country, at the summit
of the village, and the churchyard, several
times enlarged, contains still the tomb from
which the great preacher addressed the people
when the rector refused him the pulpit in
the church. Yet this famous historical monument is hard to distinguish, and of Samuel
and his children there is no memorial in the
church. As you go down the long avenue
back into the village you may easily fancy

yourself back in the eighteenth century, if not in its earliest years before the name of Wesley was one to conjure with yet in the days of George III., when such a man had no honour in his own country among his own people. But in the village itself and far around it, the chapel that bears his name will show you that his mark is stamped deep upon the land of his birth.

The pilgrims to John Wesley's birthplace very often forget that Epworth was not the only scene of his youthful activities. His father was almost as often at his other "living" as he was at Epworth, and John was, after he was grown up, for a time more constantly there. The two villages are only a few miles apart by the straight, but hardly ever direct, roads which the system of dykes has made necessary.

Hetty Wesley said of Wroot that it was "devoid of wisdom, wit, and grace". To-day the village is in outer appearance but little changed, however much it may have advanced in all these desirable qualities. The population is given as 375, larger probably than in Wesley's time. The pleasant rectory house is of the seventeenth century, and contains many features that may have been in existence when Wesley lived there, as the tradition is that he did " turn and turn about " with his father when they served the parish with that of Epworth. The church, which is modern and ugly, has an Elizabethan chalice of the familiar small type, which Wesley must often have used, and in the churchyard is the tomb of Whitelamb, his brother-in-law.

Long stretches of road between dykes lead to Misperton and Gainsborough and modern civilisation. A country in which a man should possess his soul in patience, yet where reaction might breed volcanic energy. Open to every wind of heaven and to the broad spaces of earth and sky, far from the world's disputings, a place it is in which man could often find solitude with God. No greater contrast is there in the Judæan desert where the Baptist's strength was nurtured ; yet the message of Wesley was like his, " Repent ye ", and it was heard as his was by all sorts and conditions of men.

But, perhaps, too much may be made of this out of the world influence on young John Wesley. We must not forget that though he was a Lincolnshire man by birth he was a London schoolboy. The Charterhouse was his school ; and there he had, as most boys of his time had—and indeed in the Lincoln-shire schools had much later—a hard time of it. " The tyranny of the elder boys ", in Southey's phrase, was abundantly bestowed on the poor child : his " portion of meat " was consumed by his elders, and, during the greater part of his school time, " a small daily portion of bread was his only food ". Modern-day parents who make schoolmasters' lives burdensome by complaints of their boys' food might be surprised that this child lived to be eighty-eight, and may be disposed to accept his own explanation of his good health, that he always ran round the Charterhouse garden three times every morning. There were no " organised games " in those days, and Wesley would certainly have regarded them with abhorrence. But he really was never a very healthy man, he had constant illnesses, if never a very serious one. Like all sensible men, he took care of himself, so far as it was possible to do so without inter-fering with the main object of his life. His advice to others was : " Do as much to-day as you can do without hurting yourself or dis-abling you from doing the same to-morrow ",[1] and he followed the advice himself. He knew of himself what he said to another, " You are no more at liberty to throw away your health than to throw away your life ".[2]

[1] *Works* (1771), iv. 232.        [2] Letter, July 13, 1774.

Without being anything of an athlete—
indeed the semi-professional university athlete
had not been invented in his day—John Wesley
could do most of the " out-of-door " things
that young men delight in.  He could swim
and row and fish and shoot and ride ; the
last an accomplishment which served him to
the very end of his life.  And indoors he could
dance, and he did, too, in his unconverted days,
as well as drink tea with ladies ; the last a
relaxation which he never abandoned.  One
fancies that he learnt, at last, to be a fair rider,
though he seems to have had a good many
tumbles—the horse's fault, as most poor
riders claim— ; and certainly the exercise,
though it was never undertaken for pleasure,
helped to keep him hale if not hearty for very
many years.

The record of his journeys is an astonishing
one, as the complete journal edited by the late
Dr. Nehemiah Curnock—a classic and final
edition—reveals them.  And it is the more
astonishing because of the constant attacks
of illness which mark almost every month.
Wesley had an extremely strong constitution,
it is clear, which never really suffered from
the ailments which from time to time laid
him aside.  And above all he had an over-
powering self-confidence and a most deter-

mined and masterful will. One wonders what Oliver Cromwell would have said to him if they had come into conflict—as they certainly would have done : very probably what he said to the Scottish ministers, for it is difficult to believe that Wesley ever felt himself to be mistaken. In him the mental and physical attributes were very closely allied. He dominated others, because he dominated himself ; with them it was the mind he governed, with himself the body. Determination was the most prominent of his characteristics.

That perhaps may be put down, rather than his longevity, to the Spartan fare of his childhood. But he had what, following the usage of Victorian physicians, we may call " a strong constitution ", and his brother Samuel called an " iron " one. No one subjected him to psycho-analysis, so he did not pay much attention to his feelings, or wonder whether they were physical or mental. It was not a complicated age, and he became a very straightforward man. But, as we have seen above, there were " psychic " influences in his youth which very likely may have influenced him more than he knew, though he was at school when the curious happenings disturbed the rectory at Epworth. They are worth a word or two. It was late in 1715, when " a most terrible and astonishing noise was heard by a maidservant "—it is always a maidservant who hears these things : why ?—" at the dining-room door, which caused the up-starting of her hair, and made her ears prick forth at an unusual rate ". So wrote Miss Susannah to her eldest brother Sam. The curious story is continued in the family letters, mostly addressed to Samuel, who was already a master at Westminster school, and seems to have been all through life a remarkably sensible person. There are the rappings which nowadays leave people quite calm, and the revelation of political pre-judices about which no one would now care a farthing. Nor did Sam, for he said : " As to the Devil being an enemy of King George " —the father Wesley having been a Nonjuror was rather sensitive about his new allegiance —" were I the King I should rather Old Nick be my enemy than my friend ". But even Sam felt a touch of the ghostliness : " I do not like the noise of the night gown sweeping along the ground ".[1]

When the knockings became louder and

[1] The phrase may be recommended to the Provost of Eton for the next Ghost Story of an Antiquary. The letters are very well worth reading, and may be found in Mr. Fitz-Gerald's edition of Southey's *Life*, vol. i. pp. 372-395.

more continuous the family became extremely
alarmed, and for some reason or other thought
that their father must be doomed. Mrs.
Wesley herself was not too sensible to be
frightened. As for the rector he was too
much of a bookworm to mind it all very
much. All he said was when they advised
him to resign the living—" No, let the Devil
flee from me : I will never flee from him ",
and he told the timid Suky not to be a fool.
Nothing in the end came of it all, of course ;
but Jack was made to write an account of
it, when he came home, poor boy ; and
such an impression did it make on him that
he thought it worth while to write an account
of it, years after, in the *Arminian Magazine*.
At the crisis, says Southey,[1]

" the noises were now various as well as strange, loud
rumblings above stairs or below, a clatter among a
number of bottles, as if they had all at once been
dashed to pieces, footsteps as of a man going up and
down stairs at all hours of the night, sounds like that
of dancing in an empty room the door of which was
locked, gobbling like a turkey-cock, but most frequently a knocking about the beds at night, and
in different parts of the house. Mrs. Wesley
would at first have persuaded the children and
servants that it was occasioned by rats within doors,
and mischievous persons without, and her husband
had recourse to the same ready solution : or some

[1] *Life of Wesley*, ed. FitzGerald, i. 16-17.

of his daughters, he supposed, sate up late and
made a noise ; and a hint that their lovers might
have something to do with the mystery, made the
young ladies heartily hope he might soon be convinced that there was more in the matter than he
was disposed to believe. In this they were not
disappointed, for on the next night, a little after
midnight, he was awakened by nine loud and distinct
knocks, which seemed to be in the next room, with
a pause at every third stroke. He rose and went
to see if he could discover the cause, but could
perceive nothing ; still he thought it might be some
person out of doors, and relied upon a stout mastiff
to rid them of the nuisance. But the dog, which
upon the first disturbance had barked violently, was
ever afterwards cowed by it, and seeming more
terrified than any of the children, came whining
himself to his master and mistress, as if to seek
protection in a human presence. And when the
man-servant, Robin Brown, took the mastiff at
night into his room, to be at once a guard and
companion, as soon as the latch began to jar as
usual, the dog crept into bed, and barked and
howled so as to alarm the house."

Southey's timid conclusion is that there are
more things in heaven and earth than are
dreamt of in the philosophy of " those unhappy persons who, looking through the
dim glass of infidelity, see nothing beyond the
narrow sphere of mortal existence ". No
doubt ; but that does not carry us very
far.

So John Wesley, with a good deal of
classical and theological learning, and an

interest in mathematics too, and having
" acquired some knowledge of Hebrew under
his brother Samuel's tuition "—who was
more interested in Jews than ghosts—went
up in 1720 from Charterhouse to Oxford,
and was entered at Christ Church. There
he seems to have lived a simple, unostenta-
tious life, in no way extravagant or remarkable. His parents had put before him the
thought of Holy Orders. He hesitated for
a while, as most good men do, because of
the greatness of the claim. His father seems
wisely to have put no pressure on him. His
mother was more urgent. Perhaps she was
influenced by the growing weakness of her
husband and wished John to succeed him—
for at this very time the aged rector had
written to his son : " Time has shaken me by
the hand, and Death is but a little way
behind him ".

Two books came to influence John in the
right direction, as surely they have influenced
thousands before and since, the *Imitatio
Christi* and Jeremy Taylor's *Holy Living and
Dying* ; and as their influence began to be
seen in the young man's life, " God fit you
for some great work ", said his happy
father. " Rest, watch, and pray ; believe,
love, endure, and be happy, towards which

you shall never want the most ardent prayers of your affectionate father."

John Wesley was made deacon by Bishop Potter of Oxford at the September ordination in 1725. On October 16 he preached his first sermon at South Leigh, near Witney, where still stands the fine seventeenth-century pulpit which he occupied ; and in the following spring, March 1726, he was elected Fellow of Lincoln College, which had special endowments for the county in which he was born. His father rejoiced : " What will be my own fate before the summer be over, God knows ; *sed passi graviora*, wherever I am, my Jack is Fellow of Lincoln ".

When John Wesley was ordained, the question which has so often confronted young dons met him—ought he to stay in Oxford :

As the " high priest " who had ordained him was Bishop Potter, John Wesley wrote [to] him asking whether he had, at his Ordination, engaged himself to undertake the cure of a parish. The bishop replied : " It doth not seem to me that, at your Ordination, you engaged yourself to take the cure of any parish, provided you can, as a clergyman, better serve God and His Church in your present or some other station ". This answer satisfied him, and he determined to remain at Oxford.[1]

For the present, at least, he was satisfied to

[1] Simon, *John Wesley and the Religious Societies*, p. 105.

make Lincoln College his home. There he settled down, in society more congenial, it seems, and more serious than that of Christ Church.

In the review of his life, which he wrote in May 1738, he describes the change thus :

Removing soon after to another College, I executed a resolution, which I was before convinced was of the utmost importance—shaking off at once all my trifling acquaintance. I began to see more and more the value of Time. I applied myself closer to study. I watched more carefully against actual sins ; I advised others to be religious, according to that scheme of religion by which I modelled my own life. But meeting now with Mr. Law's *Christian Perfection* and *Serious Call*, although I was much offended at many parts of both, yet they convinced me more than ever of the exceeding height and breadth and depth of the law of God. The light flowed in so mightily upon my soul, that everything appeared in a new view. I cried to God for help, and resolved not to prolong the time of obeying Him as I had never done before. And by my continued endeavour to keep His whole law, inward and outward, to the utmost of my power, I was persuaded that I should be accepted of Him, and that I was even then in a state of salvation.

He tried, in other words, to do his duty. He took up the ordinary duties of a resident Fellow : he taught " the classics " generally, and Greek in particular ; he kept up his own studies too, logic, ethics, mathematics, divinity, and added some Arabic to his Hebrew. Those were happy months, and happier still, it may be, when he fell under the influence of the beautiful theology and character of William Law, whom, though he afterwards often disagreed with, he surely never ceased to love. From time to time too, in summer vacations at least, and sometimes for longer periods, he was able to help his father at Epworth and at Wroot. Lincolnshire was closely linked to his college ; and yet he does not seem to have carried much of the interest of one to the other. So one would infer from the example which occurs most naturally to the writer of this book.

Not far from Wesley when he was at Epworth, fifteen miles at most, lived another Fellow of Lincoln College, George Hutton, who ceased to be Fellow in 1743, and was from 1742 to 1804 Rector of Gate Burton, where sixty years after his death his ghost was said still to walk. He was a studious person with a dry, serious, almost noble face, who wore a small, well-made wig. Did they ever meet in later days ? I do not find any mention of Gate Burton in *The Journal*, or any books of Wesley's in the rector's library. The Huttons who were Wesley's constant friends were no kindred of the Huttons of Gate Burton.

The years after John Wesley's ordination were spent then partly in Oxford but chiefly in Lincolnshire. He was perfecting his talent in solitude, as Goethe says, before his character was developed in the stress of life. We often see hesitations, dissatisfaction, unsettlement in these early years, never in later life. He ministered at Wroot, his infirm father doing, with his help, what he could at Epworth. Three years after his ordination as deacon he obtained priest's orders, again from Bishop Potter, to empower him for his work. He thought, and read, and visited. Then he was recalled to Oxford to be a tutor of his college; and the logical disputations which formed an important part of the not very elaborate education of that period sharpened his wits, Southey thinks, and taught him readiness of thought and speech. Before John returned to Oxford his brother Charles had come from Westminster to Christ Church, and his was a character more equable and calm, more beautiful if more " sentimental ", than that of the elder brother. Throughout life John dominated, indeed one might say domineered, over Charles ; but without the subtle influence of the latter, gentle, holy, and self-denying, John would never have seen so far into human character or come to influence it as he did. It was at this time that Charles had the chance of inheriting a kinsman's property in Ireland, and refused it : it then went to the family from which sprang the great Duke of Wellington. Had he made a different choice, says Southey, in the midst of the great deeds of the early nineteenth century, " there might have been no Methodists, the British Empire in India might still have been menaced from Sering-apatam, and the undisputed tyrant of Europe might at this time have insulted and en-dangered us on our own shores ".

For it was Charles Wesley who began Methodism. Already, in John's absence, he had brought together a body of like-minded young men, to pray together, to frequent the Sacraments, to live as the rules of the Church of England directed her children to live. John on his return was welcomed among them ; they had thought of him in his country retirement as the young Oriel men a century later thought of the brilliant John Keble working in the villages between Cotswold and Thames. And John came at once to be the director of the Holy Club, as it was already called. His accession to it was like that of Pusey, ὁ μέγας, to the writers of the " Tracts for the Times ". For he came with a weight of reputation and authority which the younger men could not possess : with a weight of seriousness which belonged to his greater years. He came back with the thought in his heart which he had received from " a serious person " in the country : " Sir, you wish to serve God and go to heaven. Remember you cannot serve Him alone : you must therefore *find* companions or *make* them : the Bible knows nothing of solitary religion." The words sank into his heart and became the motto of his life.

# CHAPTER II

## THE BEGINNINGS OF METHODISM

So John and Charles Wesley started, very humbly, piously, unconsciously, a revival of true religion in the Church of England. Oxford, no doubt, was not so dead as it has been the fashion to represent : it never is. It did not wear its heart on its sleeve : it never does. There were noisy young gentlemen who mocked at religion, and dusty old persons who despised it : there always are. But below the surface there were quiet prayerful lives of tutors, and the fresh enthusiasm of scholars ; such, to those whose eyes are open, have always been visible. The fire was still alight : doubtless, it had burnt low : it was for the Holy Club to kindle it into flame.

From the first this little body of private friends made its rule of life one strictly derived from the Bible and the Book of Common Prayer. They attended the daily services in their college chapels ; they made their communion weekly; they fasted on the days the Prayer Book set down; they visited the sick, the poor, the prisoners; they gave alms of all they possessed. Men laughed at them, but learnt from them : that is another Oxford custom, where every one laughs at the dons. Nicknames flew about : they were called " the Sacramentarians, Bible moths, the Holy, or the Godly Club ". So what began as a nickname became an honourable title, as with the Puseyites, the Tractarians. They gathered round them the like-minded and they made no distinction of classes : it may be doubted whether at Oxford sensible young men ever did. Above all they were not in the least original : Oxford men rarely are. They set themselves to obey in community the rules of the English Church ; and here they were simply following their forefathers of a generation before. Theologically John Wesley was still, like his father, a disciple of the greatest age of English divinity, a follower of the Caroline divines. This is shown, in regard to a doctrine as to which his views in later life greatly changed, by a letter to his mother written from Oxford, February 28, 1730 :

What I so much like is his [Jeremy Taylor's] account of the pardon of sins, which is the clearest

I ever met with : " Pardon of sins, in the gospel,
is sanctification. Christ came to take away our
sins, by turning every one of us from our in-
iquities. (Acts iii. 28.) And there is not in the
nature of the thing any expectation of pardon, or
sign or signification of it, but so far as the thing
itself discovers itself, as we hate sin, grow in grace,
and arrive at the state of holiness, which is also a
state of repentance and imperfection, but yet of
sincerity of heart and diligent endeavour, in the
same degree we are to judge concerning the forgiveness of sins. For indeed that is the evangelical
forgiveness, and it signifies our pardon, because it
' effects ' it, or rather it is in the nature of the
thing, so that we are to inquire into no hidden
records. Forgiveness of sins is not a secret sen-
tence, a word, or a record, but it is a state of
change effected upon us and upon ourselves ; we
are to look for it, to read it, and understand it."
In all this he appears to steer in the middle road
exactly, to give assurance of pardon to the penitent,
but to no one else.

And in practice he modelled his little
company on the rules of the good men of
fifty years before him.

It is most important in the history of
Methodism to trace the connection between
John Wesley and the religious societies of the
end of the seventeenth century. Naturally
we must start from Wesley's own statement,
published in the *London Magazine* in 1760 :

About thirty years since I met with a book
written in King William's time, called *The Country*

*Parson's Advice to his Parishioners.* [We may note, in passing, that the book was really published in Charles II.'s day, 1680.] There I read these words : " If good men of the Church will unite together in the several parts of the kingdom, disposing themselves into friendly societies, and engaging each other, in their respective combinations, to be helpful to each other in all good Christian ways, it will be the most effectual means for restoring our decaying Christianity to its primitive life and vigour, and the supporting of our tottering and sinking Church ". A few young gentlemen, then at Oxford, approved and followed the advice. They were all zealous Churchmen, and both orthodox and regular to the highest degree. For their exact regularity they were soon nicknamed Methodists. . . . Nine or ten years after many others united together in the several parts of the kingdom, engaging, in like manner, to be helpful to each other in all good Christian ways. . . . Their one design was to forward each other in true Scriptural Christianity.

As thus stated, it would seem impossible to contradict the declaration. But we must not ignore the comment of the late Dr. Overton that " there is no doubt that John Wesley intended his Societies to be an exact repetition of what was done by Beveridge, Horneck, and Smythies sixty-two years before ". Later writers, notably Dr. Simon, have laid much emphasis on the work of Anthony Horneck. Horneck, it will be remembered, was a German, as, of course, were Zinzendorf and Böhler ; and we are led to infer a much less purely English origin for the details of Wesleyan Methodist development than we have been accustomed (and are still inclined) to believe. If Wesley was much less original, and more Germanised, than has been generally supposed, it must at least be admitted that he himself was " a true-born Englishman ", and that nearly all of his helpers belonged also to our own country. If Wesley followed Horneck, it was the thoroughly Anglicised Horneck that he followed : just as English musicians for a long while very wisely followed the thoroughly English Handel. Böhler and Zinzendorf came later in Wesley's religious life. At the beginning the Holy Club was conspicuously English. There could be no more thorough John Bull than John Wesley. And the more romantic side of the national character, in its different aspects, could not be better represented than it was in Charles Wesley, George Whitefield, and James Hervey.

Let us interject a word here about the two latter. Whitefield, the greatest popular preacher of the eighteenth century, is too eminent a figure to be dealt with as a side issue in a life of Wesley. He must be mentioned again later, but here it may just be said that he was a man of genius, but of a cast diametrically opposite to that of the Wesleys. A pot-boy people rudely called him, and it is true that he never quite cast off the manners of the public-house in which he was born. He could be most sycophantically servile to persons of social dignity : Lady Huntingdon was a personage after his own heart, and he after hers. He could abuse his equals most roundly, in language which an educated or a cultivated Christian would never use. He could turn upon his friends, and speak of saints as if they were emissaries of Satan. But then he could repent. He learnt everything that was good from John Wesley : he lived to speak of him as if he was guilty of every theological and almost every moral crime. But then he could come to his senses and say, when asked whether he would meet Wesley in heaven, that he would be so far off and Wesley so near the Throne that he would hardly get a sight of him.

Wesley's relations with Whitefield will need further notice, as will the association of the brothers, and mention must be made of many other and very different disciples. But one other of the earliest members of the Holy Club, whom Southey in his account of its beginnings singles out for mention, may find place here, though this involves some anticipation of the future development of the whole movement. Southey is contemptuous of Hervey, whose works sold much more widely than his own ; so we can imagine a living novelist, more deservedly, speaking of the novels of Marie Corelli, or a living poet laureate of the effusions of Martin Tupper. Southey says he was " the author of the *Meditations*, a book which has been translated into most European languages, and for the shallowness of its matter, its superficial sentimentality, as much as for its devotional spirit, has become singularly popular ".[1] Hervey deserves, as a typical member of the Holy Club, a rather more close examination.

Like all great religious movements the Methodist revival had many and divergent offspring, not all of them legitimate. Of those which took the best of its inspiration the most important was that which became known as the Evangelical movement. Several of the leaders of this, in its early days, were Wesley's own pupils or men who had been brought directly under his influence—for the most part they were parish clergymen, and it was in the parishes, where the incumbent had felt the inspiration of the Wesleys, that the chief

[1] *Life of Wesley*, i. 35.

D

good was done.  They adhered to the forms
of the Church, and John Wesley in his revolutionary period was inclined to consider them
mere legalists ; but they had the spirit of an
Evangelist as well as a distrust of rhapsodical
or hysterical excitement.  It was one thing
to go into a parish from outside and arouse
the wonderful spiritual excitement which so
frequently accompanied the preaching of
Wesley and Whitefield : it was quite another
to have shrieks and screams, fits and collapses,
constantly breaking in upon the quiet devotion
of the parochial worship.  Wesley could go
away and leave his excitable converts to
recover their normal attitude : a parish priest
had to deal with them every day.  Thus the
most eager of the country clergy who gave
their lives to constant visitation and exhorta-
tions stood apart from the hysteria of the
Methodist mission.  Typical of such men
was the discreet and handsome, delicate and
introspective, James Hervey (1714–58), who
held two parishes in Northamptonshire divided
by the placid Nene.  He had been a pupil
of Wesley's at Oxford, and he became an
excellent parish priest, but a popular and
extravagant writer.  The *Meditations* (among
the tombs and in the flower garden) mark
almost the *nadir* of sentimental prose: no

wonder the sturdy Johnson mocked at them in his *Meditation on a Pudding*. But Hervey was a good man, though rather effeminate and self-conceited. John Ryland (1723–1792), the anabaptist divine who is said to have promoted " polite learning among the baptists and orthodox dissenters "—though the tenets of the eighteenth - century baptists would hardly fit into any scheme of orthodoxy, and they excommunicated any who communicated at the altars of the Church—was, as school-master and minister at Northampton, a neighbour, and became a most enthusiastic friend of Hervey, his book on whose *Character* (1791) is one of the most remarkable experiments in biographical hyperbole that literature has ever produced.[1] He professed to have seen the mind of his hero " gradually rising from folly to wisdom, from unbelief to faith, from enmity to love, from pride to humility, from prejudice to unbiassed integrity, from luke-warmness to zeal, from insensibility and black ingratitude to the highest thankfulness that ever dwelt in mortal breast ", till he found in him the " mirror of the divine per-fections ". The biographer asked, in a manner

[1] It is strange that this book, which is most remarkable as illustrating the influence of Methodism on Nonconformity, is not mentioned in the life of its author in the *Dictionary of National Biography*.

immortalised by Dickens half a century later,
" will proud self-righteous Pharisees read my
book ? " And he gave the answer, " No,
they will not ". It is unnecessary to dwell
upon his reasons, but a perusal of his work
justifies a wide extension of this view. But
those who wish to see what a riot Evangeli-
calism could produce may be recommended
to read its ecstatic pages, and to repress their
surprise at the assurance that Mr. Hervey's
" BIRTHDAY was celebrated by all the PRINCES
in the COURT of HEAVEN ". James Hervey
deserved a better biographer. He was
the darling of pious ladies—notably Lady
Frances Shirley—and his *Dialogues between
Theron and Aspasio* had (as Mrs. Humphry
Ward a century later said of the Book of
Daniel) " an enormous vogue ". Nothing
can better illustrate the divergence which
separated Wesley from some of his disciples,
even though they remained in the Church
to propagate views which he, gradually
beginning to stand outside, considered un-
orthodox. Hervey was a determined pleader
for " imputed righteousness ", perhaps even
the originator of the expression. Wesley
answered him and said very plainly, " The
imputed righteousness of Christ is a phrase
not scriptural. It has done immense hurt.

I have had abundant proof that the frequent use of this unnecessary phrase, instead of 'furthering men's progress in vital holiness', has made men satisfied without any holiness at all ; yea, and encouraged them to work all uncleanness with greediness." Hervey, indeed, was little better than a pure Calvinist ; and it was this savage creed which he desired to commend to " people of elegant manners and polite accomplishments ". He was deeply pained by Wesley's published criticism, and thought to answer it. As is the case with most people who do not mix freely with their kind, criticism distressed him grievously, but he did not scruple to employ the birch himself—even to the extent of finding in John Home's deplorable but extremely popular tragedy of *Douglas* a " corrupting entertainment ". John Wesley was made of much stouter stuff ; and if all the Evangelical clergy of " the Establishment " had been as weak as Hervey, he would have swept them all ultimately into his net. Hervey died in early middle life, and the popularity of his theology did not very long survive him.

To return to the Holy Club in 1730 : many of its members lived to be, in different ways, leaders of religion. There was Benjamin Ingham who went with Wesley to America, and ended by marrying Lady Margaret Hastings, sister-in-law of that woman-pope Lady Huntingdon ; Gambold, a rather tedious person, who became a bishop among the Moravians ; Clayton, who became famous at Manchester ; William Morgan, a beloved young man, who at last lost his wits and never recovered the savage remedies of the time. Of these, Clayton was the most loyal to the Church, and he became associated with the Nonjuring Bishop, Thomas Deacon,[1] " whose ideas ", says a Methodist writer, " on most important questions were entirely anti-Protestant ".[2] Much though these young men differed in after life, they would probably all have agreed with what Hervey, some years later than the Oxford days, wrote to Wesley : " Assure yourself, dear sir, that I can never forget the tender-hearted and generous Fellow of Lincoln, who condescended to take such compassionate notice of a poor undergraduate, whom almost everybody condemned, and when no man cared for my soul ".

Thus the Holy Club attracted to itself from the first the weak as well as the strong. The Wesleys sought to brace the characters of the former by the discipline in which the

---

[1] See the admirable life of him by T. Broxap.
[2] *New History of Methodism*, i. 148.

latter found the milk of lions : they lived by
rule, " piling up the very fragments of their
time, that not a moment of it might be lost ".
The Society received the Bishop's sanction
in visiting the prisons : and John Wesley
himself began a personal association with
William Law, from whose beautiful life and
wise sayings he might have learnt, one feels,
more than he ever fully appreciated. " We
shall do well to aim at the highest degree of
perfection ", said Law, " if we may thereby
at least attain to mediocrity." And so Wesley
aimed. " You would have a philosophical
religion, but there can be no such thing.
Religion is the most plain, simple thing in
the world. This only, *We love Him, because
He first loved us.*" How well Law knew how
to speak to a college don ! And Wesley
took the saying to his heart. And there was
further advice, later, which was not so well
heeded.

MY DEAR FRIEND—You reverse matters from their
proper order. You are to follow the Divine Light,
wherever it leads you, in all your conduct. It is
God alone that gives the blessing. I pray you
always mind your own work, and go on with
cheerfulness ; and God, you may depend upon it,
will take care of His. Besides, Sir, I perceive you
would fain convert the world ! But you must wait
God's own time. Nay, if after all He is pleased
to use you only as a hewer of wood or a drawer

of water, you should submit—yea, you should be grateful to Him that He has honoured you so far.

Law was right.  Indeed the life of such a society as the Holy Club, whether it be set up in a monastery, a college, a clergy house, or an industrial centre, is doomed to hours of disappointment.  Such the Wesleys experienced after they had been home, hoping that all would go well in their absence.  Says Dr. Simon in the earliest portion of his great study of Wesley : [1]

On their return to Oxford in May 1731 they found that the " Holy Club " was threatened with extinction.  The little company that used to meet on a Sunday evening was " shrunk into almost nothing at all ".  [It had once numbered twenty-seven : it shrank to five.]  It appeared as if the attrition of time would accomplish more than the assaults of Oxford opponents.  Their opposition, however, was maintained, and John Wesley had often cause to admit the truth of a saying of Dr. Hayward's when he examined him for priest's Orders :  " Do you know what you are about ? You are bidding defiance to all mankind.  He that would live a Christian priest ought to know that, whether his hand be against every man or no, he must expect every man's hand should be against him."  Towards the close of the year, the sorely tried brothers were encouraged by a visit from their father, who saw the work they were doing, and in a letter to his wife told her of the " shining piety "

[1] *Wesley and the Religious Societies*, p. 95.

of their two sons. And he said, " I hear my son has the honour of being styled the Father of the Holy Club : if it be so I am sure I must be the grandfather of it, and I need not say that I had rather any of my sons should be so dignified and distinguished, than to have the title of His Holiness."

But already the ways of the family were beginning to diverge. Samuel, the sensible one, left Westminster and went to be head master at Tiverton. Samuel, the father, began visibly to fail, and he urged his son to apply in advance for the next presentation to his living. This was not thought to be wrong in those days, or later : even Edward Bouverie Pusey asked for the Regius Professorship of Divinity : the feeling that " those who don't ask don't want " is supposed still to linger in clerical circles. But John Wesley did not ask, and soon found that he did not want. He fancied that without the spiritual privileges of Oxford, though he might preach to others he himself would be a castaway. In fact he had tried the country parson's life and he could not face it again. In truth he was all for a bustle ; a quiet life was not for him ; he must live among thinking men, and congenial, and, if it might be, subservient companions. He longed for " a wider sphere " in the cant phrase of later days. And his bishop supported him. " It doth not seem to me ", he said, " that, at your ordination, you engaged yourself to undertake the care of any parish, provided you can, as a clergy-man, better serve God and His Church in your present or some other station." Much the same has often been said to themselves by those who have become bishops ; also by those who have become heresiarchs. Wesley was already on the way to taking the world for his parish. He had not learnt, and perhaps never did learn, the lesson of the ancient writer that " the very beginning of wisdom is the desire of discipline ". Wesley was soon to have the opportunity of learning this. It cannot be said that he took it.

In April 1785 Samuel Wesley the elder died at Epworth, " ripe for immortality ". John and Charles were with him at the end. He left behind him nothing but debts and his lucubrations on Job. The latter were to be presented by John to Queen Caroline, who delighted to discuss theology and German metaphysics, patronised Socinians or Uni-tarians, and rescued Joseph Butler from the country, where he was " not dead but buried ". The visit to London was the first of the great turning points of John's life. He heard of the great colonising scheme of General Oglethorpe, and how that good man wanted missionaries for the settlers and the Indians. His heroic mother looked up out of her poverty and loneliness and said, " Had I twenty sons, I should rejoice that they were all so employed, though I should never see them more ". Sensible Samuel was against the project : he thought it the duty of his brothers to stay at home. But John and Charles heeded him not : they not often did. They gave up the Holy Club at Oxford and sailed for America on October 14, 1735.

Here begins that wonderful journal which for nearly sixty years lets posterity into the very soul of this devoted man. John Wesley is as candid as Pepys. Pepys certainly never wrote for publication, and probably it was some years before Wesley did. On the American journey indeed he stripped his soul quite bare, and had no eye to the future when he set down in writing his doings and his thoughts.

Two points emerge from a study of Wesley's American experiences—two points beyond the one aim which guided all his life, to serve God and bring men to His love and forgiveness. Both show a lack of discipline, which the rules of the Holy Club had not been able to instil. The first is a certain restlessness of mind, the second a self-opinionated intolerance of spirit. The first was brought out by the companionship of twenty-six Moravians on board the ship which took him across the Atlantic. He studied them with the same closeness with which R. L. Stevenson, the Amateur Emigrant, observed his professional companions. He learnt a great deal from them in piety and self-denial. He learnt something of the devouring enthusiasm of Zinzendorf of Herrnhut, the " banished Count ". At first this profoundly unsettled him. He was never content to take God's guidance without interrogation. He loved to choose and see his path. He was panting for some definite assurance before he could say with his whole heart, " Lead Thou me on ". To some men God's all - embracing goodness gives this : to some His wisdom denies it. To the Moravians it seemed to be the first step on the way to salvation, the essential step. Wesley knew no assurance yet, and the passages in his *Journal* where his experiences are recorded were written in the very bitterness of his soul.

The sea voyage was a long one. It was not until February 6, 1736, that the travellers landed at Savannah. General Oglethorpe in his colony of Georgia was a leader of wise and religious foresight, and his work is one of the brightest episodes in the story of American beginnings. Southey [1] thinks he committed two errors : he introduced something like a feudal system of land-tenure :

And the importation of rum was prohibited : it is said that this spirit, when properly diluted, is proved by experience to be the wholesomest and most refreshing drink, as well as the cheapest for workmen in that foggy and burning climate ; and it is certain that to forbid the use of a thing good in itself because it is liable to be abused, is subjecting the worthy part of the community to a privation for the sake of the worthless.

This is Southey's complaint. In the copy which Samuel Taylor Coleridge profusely annotated there is no comment. But these difficulties were not such as would disturb the Wesleys.

Soon after they landed John went one way and Charles another. The younger proved himself gracious and humble. The elder was intolerant and autocratic. He forgot his Church history, or had never read it with intelligence. The latter, indeed, when we consider his subsequent career, is the more probable supposition. Anyhow he would not admit the baptism of any who had

[1] Vol. i. p. 63.

not received the Sacrament from Episco-
palians ; and he turned away from the altar
some whom he had no Christian right to reject.
He soon set a whole congregation by the
ears. And perhaps worst of all he was
extraordinarily silly, tiresome and uncharit-
able, in regard to a very agreeable but
rather frightened and fickle young lady.

Neither of the Wesleys had as yet obtained much experience of the habits and
tastes of the fair sex. Oxford students of
that age never did : the reverse is very much
the case now. Thus one need not be surprised that even the gentle and reasonable
Charles began by some bad mistakes. He
attempted, says Southey,[1] " the doubly difficult task of reforming some of the lady
colonists, and reconciling their petty jealousies
and hatreds of each other ; in which he
succeeded no further than just to make them
cordially agree in hating him and caballing
to get rid of him in any way ". He was a
very good but never a very wise man, and
now he was a young man too. Without
believing that the colonists were generally of
the nature of Mr. Ducat and the ladies in
Gay's *Polly*, we may be quite sure that there
were some very bad, some very careless, and

[1] Vol. i. p. 68.

some very irritable folk among them. Charles could not say his prayers in the open air, in an innocent grove of myrtles, without being shot at ; and even Oglethorpe thought him indiscreet and troublesome and treated him, it seems, with harshness foreign to his nature. " Woe is me that I am constrained to dwell with Mesech," said poor Charles.

But two good men could not long be kept apart, and when John came to see his brother (having rolled overboard on the way, and awoke to find himself under water, but unconcernedly swum round the ship and swarmed up a rope on to the deck), and soon all was well, he proved, for once, a reconciling force. Oglethorpe gave Charles a diamond ring (which Charles, with the propriety which marked clergymen of those days, would never wear) and " embraced and kissed him with the most cordial affection ". All was well, and before long Charles returned to the work he was much better fitted for in England.

Now John was of much sterner stuff ; but he was also much more impetuous and indiscreet. Sophia Hopkey, the governor's niece, had " fixed her eyes on " him. She " was introduced to him as one suffering under a wounded spirit " : when he was ill

in bed she tended him night and day : he
accepted her attentions and gave her perhaps
sound but certainly irritating advice, such as
" to sup earlier and not immediately before
she went to bed ". She bore the advice
meekly, and continued what Wesley's friend
Delamotte described as her artfulness. Wesley
then consulted his Moravian pope, who had
a conclave of the elders on the subject ;
and all advised him " to proceed no further
in this business ".[1] The quotation from
*Macbeth* need not necessarily suggest that
they regarded marriage as harshly as murder.
But Miss Sophia Hopkey no doubt got wind
of it and married some one else. God,
thought Wesley (June 4, 1737), showed him
the greatness of his deliverance and opened
to him a new and unexpected scene of Miss
Sophy's dissimulation. After this it would
have been best to let well alone ; but that
Wesley could never do. He reproved the
lady for conduct which he thought blame-
worthy : he proceeded to refuse to her the
Holy Communion. " The next day [August
7, 1737] a warrant was issued against him for
defaming Sophia Williamson and refusing to
administer to her the Sacrament of the Lord's
Supper in a public congregation without

[1] *Journal*, i. 315, Curnock's notes.

cause." Very soon other matters of complaint, which had long been rankling, were tacked on, and Wesley was indicted for having " broken the laws of the realm, contrary to the peace of our Sovereign Lord the King, his crown and dignity ". Out of the mighty fuss that ensued, as the weeks stretched into months, Wesley thought the only wise thing to do was to run. Therefore, after adventures which suggest those of Stevenson's Fair Cuban, he fled. He had a horrible voyage : the sea and the waves roared and his heart failed him for fear—not physical, of which he was ever quite incapable, but mental and spiritual. " I went to America to convert the Indians : but oh ! who shall convert me ? "

The answer was not long delayed. On February 3, 1738, Wesley arrived in London : two days later he preached at S. John's, Westminster, in a style so " light-strained " as to receive a warning that he must not preach there again. In truth a spiritual crisis had come, and the Moravians were those who should guide him through it. " What can I preach ? " said Wesley in the depth of his spiritual distress. "Preach faith", replied Böhler, " till you have it, and then because you have it you will preach faith." He acted

E

upon the advice, and one of the first things
he did (May 14, 1738) was to reproach the
saintly William Law for not having told him
plainly " Believe in the Lord Jesus Christ
and nothing shall be impossible to thee.
Strip thyself naked of thy own works and
thy own righteousness and flee to Him."
How would Law answer to their common
Lord that he never so advised him—" Why
did I scarcely ever hear you name the name
of Christ, never so as to found anything upon
faith in His blood ? " Law's was a very
wise answer : it reminded Wesley of all he
should have learnt from the *Imitatio Christi* ;
it gave the very necessary caution : " The
head can as easily amuse itself with a *living
and justifying faith in the blood of Jesus* as
with any other notion ; and the heart, which
you suppose to be a place of beauty, as being
the place of self love, is more deceitful than
the head ".

But John was on the way to a change
which psycho-analysts would probably tell
us was already anticipated by his complex.
Charles, dangerously ill and recovering, had
already found rest for his soul. John, on
May 24, 1730, attended a Moravian meeting
in Aldersgate Street, and suddenly, he says,
" an assurance was given me, that He had

taken away *my* sins, even *mine*, and saved me from the law of sin and death ".

The Holy Club had provided an organisation of Methodism : now it received a theology.

# CHAPTER III

SINCE brother Samuel had left London for Tiverton his house in Dean's Yard had been occupied by certain good folk named Hutton, who were deeply religious people, and, in the language of the time, Church of England men not fanatics. The brothers John and Charles were always at home there. And there it was, on May 20, 1738, that John, whose goodness they had so long known and loved, who was since he returned from America a most famous and much sought after preacher, astonished his host by declaring that he had never been a Christian till five days before. Hutton implored him to beware lest he despise the benefits of the two Sacraments, and his wife more directly replied : " If you were not a Christian ever since I knew you, you were a great hypocrite, for you made us all believe you were one ". When Hutton spoke of the Sermon on the Mount, Wesley's strange retort was : " It is the letter that killeth ".

As usual, the sensible Samuel was appealed to by the friends, who were alarmed at the fanaticism or " enthusiasm " which seemed to them now to dominate the mind of John. And he answered them as sensibly as ever : [1]

What Jack means by his not being a Christian till last month, I understand not. Had he never been in covenant with God ? Then, as Mr. Hutton observed, baptism was nothing. Had he totally apostatized from it ? I dare say not ; and yet he must either be unbaptized, or an apostate, to make his words true. Perhaps it might come into his crown that he was in a state of mortal sin unrepented of, and had long lived in such a course. This I do not believe : however, he must answer for himself. But where is the sense of requiring everybody else to confess that of themselves, in order to commence Christians ? Must they confess it whether it be so or no ? Besides, a sinful course is not an abolition of the covenant ; for that very reason, because it is a breach of it. If it *were* not, it would not be *broken*.

But, before he knew of this letter, John Wesley's course was decided on. He had received an illuminating thought, like S. Augustine, or S. Francis, or Martin Luther ; and he was determined to act upon it. He knew in his heart that the Moravians were at least the channels of the message which came to him, he believed, from God. He

[1] Southey, *Life of Wesley*, vol. i. p. 120.

determined to see how this doctrine of theirs, which in truth was Luther's, was worked out in their lives. He must see the Moravians at home. He went to Herrnhut.

, Though the Moravian teaching, which was in its essence Lutheran, was the ground-work on which Wesley's conversion, assurance, and subsequent theology were all based, its system and its leaders had no permanent influence upon him. It may therefore, in so short a biography as this, speedily be dismissed. Briefly, it traces its history partly to Hus and his followers, partly to Comenius in the seventeenth century. Its method of government is regarded as Episcopal, its theology is certainly Protestant of the Lutheran type. It lays great stress upon the education of the young, in which at one time it may be said to have been the worthy rival of the Jesuits or the Port Royalists. Early in the eighteenth century the Moravians obtained a great accession of strength through the adhesion of Nicholas Louis, Count Zinzendorf, a sort of earlier and more definitely Christian Tolstoi. Zinzendorf was admitted to the Protestant ministry at Tübingen, and to the Moravian episcopate at Berlin. Potter, now Archbishop of Canterbury, recognised his position and welcomed his missionary work in Georgia. When he came to Germany, Wesley learnt much from him, and more from the abler thinker Peter Böhler; and he wrote to his brother Samuel: " I am with a Church whose conversation is in heaven ". But he soon found Zinzendorf too much of an autocrat and too little of a theologian. Southey tells a story of his experience there; but evidently without believing it.[1]

Mr. Hampson, in his *Life of Wesley*, relates that the Count, who regarded him as a pupil, ordered him one day to dig in the garden. " When Mr. Wesley had been there some time, working in his shirt, and in a high perspiration, he called upon him to get into a carriage that was in waiting, to pay a visit to a German Count; nor would he suffer him either to wash his hands, or to put on his coat. ' You must be simple, my brother! ' was a full answer to all his remonstrances; and away he went like a crazed man *in statu quo*." Mr. Hampson adds that he has no doubt of the authenticity of this anecdote; but it is not likely that Zinzendorf, who had been in England, should have exacted this proof of docility from an English clergyman, nor that Wesley should have submitted to it. Similar, but more extravagant, tales are common in monastic history.

He soon found also, as Southey says, that there was " as little personal liberty at Herrnhut as in a convent, and less than in a Jesuit

[1] Vol. i. p. 137.

Reduction ". And personal liberty was the
very breath of life to John Wesley. With
his heart full of love for their goodness he
returned to London and straightway set to
work to explain to them their errors. He
addressed to the Moravian Church in September 1738 a series of most searching questions :
the most important of all was " Is not the
Count all in all ? Are not the rest mere
shadows, calling him Rabbi ; almost im-
plicitly both believing and obeying him."
*De te fabula narratur* men might have said to
himself : for the Methodists in a few years
became Wesleyans, and the change of title
meant a real change of outlook. It was not
long before Zinzendorf and Wesley parted.
At first the Methodist had seemed to be an
offshoot of the Moravians ; but when it was
seen that Zinzendorf regarded himself as their
Pope, and even before their " extravagances "
had been imported into England, Wesley,
with much sorrow of heart no doubt, had cast
off those from whom he had learnt so much.
By 1744, after an interview between Wesley
and Zinzendorf, there was an open rupture.
Wesley saw in their theology, and in the
excesses to which he believed it gave rise, a
violent divergence from the faith he had
believed.

He wrote vehemently as to the teaching: [1]

Having procured a sight of that amazing com-
pound of nonsense and blasphemy, the last hymn-
book published by Count Zinzendorf's Brethren,
I believed it was my bounden duty to transcribe
a few of those wonderful hymns, and publish them
to all the world, as a standing proof that there is
no folly too gross for those who are wise above
that is written.

The excesses cannot be denied, but there
came to be Wesleyan excesses (much less
heinous) too. One is sometimes reminded of
that chapter of Voltaire's on the later develop-
ments of Port Royal. The theological divergence is not great; it has been flippantly
compared to that in music between Handel
and Buononcini.

> Strange that such difference should be
> 'Twixt Tweedledum and Tweedledee.

More serious persons may find comfort in
the conclusion of S. T. Coleridge : " In the
present instance the parties could not but
misunderstand each other; for Zinzendorf
was a theosopher or Cabiric metaphysician
without logic, and Wesley a logician without
metaphysics ".

It was not long after his return to England
that the real lifework of John Wesley began.

[1] *Journal*, Thursday, December 15, 1748.

His brother Charles, already in London, had
been following the steps of the Oxford Holy
Club.   He had been visiting the prisoners in
Newgate, and there John joined him, and
with the beautiful sincerity and unflinching
courage which marked them they brought
many sinners to a knowledge of the love of
God and the peace that passeth all understanding.   Here was the real *motif* of the
lives of these two noble brothers : all through
the tangle of their theology and the incon-
sistencies of their conduct there runs the
master passion of the love of souls.   It is
that which makes them immortal among the
Englishmen who have served their country
and loved the Lord Jesus Christ.

They were anxious from the first to act
under the authority of the Church whose
ministers they were.   Thus, on October 20,
1738, they called upon Bishop Gibson of
London, the most learned and temperate
bishop of the day.   This wise man put before
them a definition of assurance which they
were forced to accept, though, if not already
yet soon, they went beyond it.   They admitted that they had rebaptized those who
had been baptized by dissenters.

" Who gave you authority to baptize ? "
—" Your lordship," replied Charles (for he

had been ordained priest by him), " and I shall exercise it in any part of the known world."—" Are you a licensed curate ? " said the bishop, who began to feel justly offended at the tenor of this conversation ; and Charles Wesley, who then perceived that he could no longer appeal to the letter of the law, replied he had the leave of the proper minister.—" But do you not know that no man can exercise parochial duty in London without my leave ? It is only *sub silentio*." —" But you know many do take that permission for authority, and you yourself allow it."—" It is one thing to connive," said the bishop, " and another to approve ; I have power to inhibit you."—" Does your lordship exact that power ? Do you now inhibit me ? " The answer was : " Oh ! why will you push matters to an extreme ? " and the bishop put an end to this irritating interview by saying : " Well, sir, you knew my judgement before and you know it now ".[1]

They went on to Bishop Potter. John Wesley, whom he had ordained, thought him a " great and good man ", yet hardly took to heart his wise advice—" If you desire to be extensively useful, do not spend your time and strength in contending for or against

[1] Southey, vol. i. p. 157.

such things as are of a disputable nature ; but in testifying against open notorious vice, and in promoting real essential holiness ". How often has this advice been given to deaf ears !

But Wesley thought he could do both : fight for a theology that was disputatious or at least disputable, and by it convert sinners to holiness. " God deliver me and all that seek Him in sincerity from what the world calls *Christian prudence* ! "

Now Whitefield, who had even more of enthusiastic fire than John Wesley, returned from Georgia and was ordained priest by Bishop Benson of Gloucester (January 14, 1739). On New Year's Day, in the room in Fetter Lane where they were accustomed to assemble, sixty of the brethren who followed their teaching assembled with the Wesleys, Whitefield, Hall, Kinchin, Ingham, and Hutchins, and continued all night in prayer, filled with a Pentecostal sense of the presence of God. It may well be that here, as Southey thinks, was the origin of the famous field preaching.[1]

Meetings of this kind prolonged far into the midnight and even through the night were what neither the Wesleys nor Whitefield approved in

[1] Vol. i. p. 163.

their cooler age. They gave just offence to the
better part of the clergy ; and men who were
neither deficient in piety nor in zeal properly
refused to lend their pulpits to preachers who
seemed to pride themselves upon setting prudence
at defiance. But if this had not driven them to
field-preaching, they would have taken to that
course, from a necessity of a different nature. One
Sunday, when Whitefield was preaching at Ber-
mondsey Church, as he tells us, " with great freedom
in his heart, and clearness in his voice ", to a
crowded congregation, near a thousand people
stood in the churchyard during the service, hundreds
went away who could not find room, and he had
a strong inclination to go out and preach to them
from one of the tombstones. " This ", he says,
" put me first upon thinking of preaching without
doors. I mentioned it to some friends, who looked
upon it as a mad notion. However, we knelt
down and prayed that nothing may be done rashly.
Hear and answer, O Lord, for Thy Name's sake ! "

On February 17 Whitefield began his
wonderful open-air mission, and Kingswood,
a settlement of colliers near Bristol, was
the scene of what seemed a life-giving in-
novation. Such, of course, it was not ;
preaching in the open air had been quite
common before the Reformation and after
it : Paul's Cross and Magdalen College,
Oxford, stood as witnesses. But in the
comfortable eighteenth century it seemed
unpleasant ; to those who remembered In-
dependency and Quakerism and the Scottish

Covenanters it seemed illegal; and to those who lived on pew rents it seemed dangerous.

Whitefield, happy in the results of his departure from convention, entreated the Wesleys to join him at Bristol, and an excellent young layman, Mr. Seward of Everham (whom one cannot but believe to have afforded the groundwork for Richard Graves's acute and diverting Spiritual Quixote), urged them to comply with the request. They delayed; consulted the Bible in their quaint and superstitious way, as Charles I. had done before them, in *sortes Virgilianae*; found contradictory suggestions; hesitated; and went. John Wesley was first shocked at field preaching, then interested, then argumentative (with himself), then convinced. And so he says: " I submitted to be more vile and proclaimed in the highways the glad tidings of salvation, speaking from a little eminence in a ground adjoining to the city to about three thousand people ".

There were startling results: shrieks, groans, foamings, faintings, struggles, agonies of remorse, paroxysms of joy; but there is no more glorious scene in English history than that of the Methodists preaching Christ at Kingswood while tears made white furrows on the colliers' grimy cheeks. So Methodism as a converting world-force began.

Thus John wrote to his brother Samuel : [1]

"My dear Brother," he says, "the whole question turns on matter of fact. You deny that God does now work these effects ; at least that He works them in such a manner. I affirm both, because I have heard those facts with my ears, and seen them with my eyes. I have seen (as far as it can be seen) many persons changed in a moment from the spirit of horror, fear, and despair to the spirit of hope, joy, peace ; and from sinful desires, till then reigning over them, to a pure desire of doing the will of God. These are matters of fact, whereof I have been, and almost daily am, eye or ear witness. Upon the same evidence (as to the suddenness and reality of the change) I believe, or know this, touching visions and dreams ; I know several persons in whom this great change, from the power of Satan unto God, was wrought either in sleep, or during a strong representation to the eye of their minds of Christ, either on the cross, or in glory. This is the fact ; let any judge of it, as they please. But that such a change was then wrought appears, not from their shedding tears only, or sighing, or singing psalms, but from the whole tenour of their life, till then in many ways wicked, from that time holy, just, and good. I will show you him that was a lion till then, and is now a lamb ; he that was a drunkard, but now exemplarily sober ; the whoremonger that was, who now abhors the very lusts of the flesh. These are my living arguments for what I assert, that God now, as aforetime, gives remission of sins, and the gift of the Holy Ghost, which may be called visions.

[1] Letter in Southey, vol. i. p. 182.

If it be not so, I am found a false witness ; but, however, I do and will testify the things I have both seen and heard."

But the elder brother, to whom such experiences were unknown, remained detached. John Wesley determined to stay at Bristol and pursue the good work. It was with no hardness of heart that he resisted the appeals of his brother Samuel to visit him. He was so absorbed in his mission that he did not see how near at hand was death ; it came on November 5 of that year. The brothers were controverting each other's theology almost to the end. And Samuel had the sorrow of knowing that his good mother had " countenanced a spreading delusion, so far as to be one of Jack's congregation ". She had accepted the doctrine of Assurance as John preached it ; it seemed to her to come, at the moment of communion, as a special revelation from God. At the moment when he tells of the sad separation between brothers, which, indeed, one feels, a personal meeting might speedily have ended, Southey stays us from harshly condemning the great evangelist by quoting some words of his old age :

When fifty years ago my brother Charles and I, in the simplicity of our hearts, told the good

people of England that unless they knew their sins
were forgiven they were under the wrath and curse
of God, I marvel they did not stone us ! The
Methodists, I hope, know better now. We preach
assurance, as we always did, as a common privilege
of the children of God ; but we do not enforce it,
under the pain of damnation enforced on all who
enjoy it not.

That surely was what his mother meant :
that surely would have satisfied the devout
wisdom of her eldest son.

But still the Moravian influence remained
powerful over John Wesley. It was indeed
permanent, and what it was has never been
better expressed than by an eminent secular
historian :

" From Böhler ", says Mr. Lecky, " he first
learned to believe that every man, no matter how
moral, how pious, or how orthodox he may be, is
in a state of damnation, until by a supernatural
and instantaneous process wholly unlike that of
human reasoning, the conviction flashes upon his
mind that the sacrifice of Christ has been applied
to him, and has expiated his sins ; that this super-
natural and personal conviction or illumination is
what is meant by Saving Faith, and that it is in-
separably accompanied by an absolute assurance of
Salvation, and by a complete domination over sin.
It cannot exist where there is not a sense of pardon
of all past and of freedom from all present sins. It
is impossible that he who had experienced it should
be in serious and lasting doubt as to the fact, for its
fruits are constant peace—not one uneasy thought."[1]

[1] Lecky, *History*, ii. 556-557.

F

Such was the vital conviction of the first Methodists, and this enabled the body to survive the troubles of its early years.

Like all great movements the Evangelical Revival had to pass through a period of confusion and violence. The first years of Wesleyanism are full of the most painful extravagances and frenzies, which John records in his *Journal* sadly, soberly, sometimes sardonically. He hoped that they would fall off as the movement rose to its full strength. And the first step towards that seemed, sad though it was, to be the separation of the Wesleys from Whitefield.

# CHAPTER IV

## DIVISION AND DEFINITION

AT least from 1739 it must have become
evident that the movement led by the Wesleys
would make a permanent mark on the Church.
They had already a large number of devoted
followers : their work was beginning to be
known all over England : it excited alarm
and criticism as well as gratitude and enthusiasm. And John Wesley had become recognised as a great preacher, and was proving
himself to be a born leader of men.

The results were inevitable. Methodism,
with its roots in the past, had its mission for
the future.

Beginning with an imitation of the seventeenth-century Religious Societies, the work
of the Wesleys and of Methodism led slowly,
gradually, even hesitatingly to the foundation
of a new Society, of which it has been said
that while John Wesley was "a firm believer
in the doctrines of the Church of England

which relate to the salvation of the individual",
he saw that " a new beginning had to be made,
a Society on a simpler basis had to be formed,
a Society whose supreme work was ' to spread
Scriptural holiness over the land ' ".

This final achievement, disruption, separation was very slowly reached ; but, as the
movement advanced, it was inevitable that it
should involve separation among those who
had at first been of kin to it but in practice
rather than in theory, for every great movement must have a theory behind it. And
this separation would necessarily involve
definition. Wesley had to state what he did
not believe and what he did believe. The
movement had to make plain, in the language
of a much later generation, what it stood for.

Protestantism, it has often been said, has
an inherent tendency to multiply separation.
The insistence upon articles as essential to
Christianity which go beyond the ancient
definitions inevitably leads to division. " Now
the Catholic faith is this : that we worship
one God in Trinity and the Trinity in Unity ":
that, with the noble protest of Archbishop
Laud, directed primarily against the contro-
versial Romanist, but of much wider applica-
tion, forms a foundation upon which the
Church of England at least, as a part of

Christ's Holy Catholic Church, may securely
rest.  Said Laud, " I will never take on me
to express that tenet or opinion, the denial
of the foundation only excepted, which may
shut any Christian, even the meanest, out of
heaven ".[1]

The enthusiastic Whitefield, carried away
by the successes of his own eloquence, thought
otherwise and much less wisely :  so, it seems,
came to think John Wesley.   And it is curious
that Wesley, like Laud, was called an Arminian.   That is to say both these great Englishmen rejected the Calvinism which seemed to
the more impetuous Whitefield to flow from
the doctrine of perfection, which Wesley,
taking his theology from Protestant not
Catholic sources, had adopted.   Wesley knew
" that Whitefield held the Calvinistic tenets
of election and irreversible decrees ;  tenets
which, if true, would make God unjust and
the whole Gospel a mere mockery ", says
Southey.   " *Which seem, prima facie*, to make "
—corrects Coleridge more charitably, for he
thinks the doctrine is harmless, because (one
supposes) really meaningless unless mixed
with the poison of the doctrine of individual
assurance.   Harmless it may be to the character of the individual, but not so to a belief in a

---

[1] *Works*, i. 60.

righteous God. This Wesley saw very clearly.
His theology was unalterably opposed to that
of Calvin. Whitefield was as determined on
the other side. God, he said, taught all his
friends the " Doctrine of Election ", and he
urged his dear and honoured Mr. Wesley to
join with them. With the freedom of anticipation which coloured his theology so deeply,
he assured his honoured friend and brother
that he would know on the Judgement Day
that " sovereign, distinguishing, irresistible
grace " brought him to heaven ; and he
entreated his friends to prevent Wesley disputing with him. Wesley showed the strong
common sense which never deserted him. It
was long before the Calvinistic Methodists
could draw from him any word of condemna-
tion. There was a typical scene on June 19,
1740, when a member of the Society named
Acourt proclaimed his Calvinism publicly.

John was present when next he presented
himself and demanded whether they refused admitting a person only because he differed from them
in opinion. Wesley answered No, but asked what
opinion he meant. He replied, " That of election.
I hold that a certain number are elected from
eternity, and these must and shall be saved, and
the rest of mankind must and shall be damned."
And he affirmed that many of the Society held the
same ; upon which Wesley observed that he never
asked whether they did or not ; " only let them

not trouble others by disputing about it ".  Acourt
replied, " Nay, but I will dispute about it."  " Why
then ", said Wesley, " would you come among us,
who you know are of another mind ? "  " Because
you are all wrong, and I am resolved to set you all
right."  " I fear ", said Wesley, " your coming
with this view would neither profit you nor us."
" Then ", rejoined Acourt, " I will go and tell all
the world that you and your brother are false
prophets. And I tell you in one fortnight you
will all be in confusion." [1]

Wesley published a sermon, temperate
enough : but Whitefield would not listen.
He was indeed theologically the most intem-
perate of men, and words of abuse flew from
his mouth swift as an arrow from a Tartar's
bow. " The Devil rages in London. He
begins now to triumph indeed," he said : a
far from kindly allusion to the moderation of
his first teacher. Then, after the manner of
such men, he published what Wesley had
told him about his decision being taken after
drawing lots : he derided the weakness of his
honoured friend. His language became hysterical, almost nauseous : it is the common
danger of popular rhetoricians when they de-
scend from the pulpit. But Wesley remained
more than usual calm : he did not say one
single word of reproach. Only he repeated
trenchantly, " The sum of all is this : one

[1] Vol. i. p. 264.

in twenty (suppose) of mankind are *elected* ;
nineteen in twenty are *reprobated* ! The
elect shall be saved, *do what they will* ; the
reprobate shall be damned, *do what they can*."
That certainly, whether it be true Calvinism
or no, certainly is not Christianity : and
Southey's words are not too strong for such
an opinion. " This is the doctrine of Calvinism, for which Diabolism would be a better
name ; and in the worst and bloodiest idolatry
that ever defiled the earth there is nothing so
horrid, so monstrous, so impious as this." It
is not only preachers who can use strong
language. Still Wesley did not speak. When
Whitefield, or his friends, published and distributed a letter which he had written to his
old teacher, in which ecstatic praise did not
disguise the bitter attack, all Wesley did was
to tear it in pieces before those to whom he
was preaching, saying he was sure Whitefield,
were he present, would do the same. And
when still baser treachery assailed him from
others, all he did was to declare that they no
longer belonged to the Society. During part
of this time Whitefield was in America. When
he returned he was as personally affectionate
as ever, but, theologically, as unyielding.
Wesley seemed in danger of being bereft of
all his friends : even Charles for a time seemed

inclined to draw away, in sympathy with the Moravians. But between those who loved each other so much there could be no long disunion. Wesley rose above it, and set himself, with the discrimination of a master mind, to perfect the organisation of the body he had founded.

The creation of two magazines, each to expound the views of its parties and to attack those of the other, marked the period of definite division between Wesley and White-field. Wesley's was called the *Arminian Magazine*, Whitefield's the *Gospel Magazine*. Before long there was a good deal of bitterness displayed. But at first Wesley was reticent, at least in his public teaching. In a letter dated November 1774 he wrote that :

In public preaching speak not one word against opinions of any kind. We are not to fight against notions, but sins. Least of all should I advise you once to open your lips against *Predestination*. It would do more mischief than you are aware of. Keep to our one point, present inward salvation by faith, by the divine evidence of sins forgiven.

In practice the organisation of his Society grew. On April 9, 1743, he writes in his *Journal* :

We had the first watch-night in London. We commonly choose for this solemn service the Friday night nearest the full moon, either before or after, that those of the congregation who live at a distance may have light to their several homes. The service begins at half an hour past eight, and continues till a little after midnight. We have often found a peculiar blessing at these seasons. There is generally a deep awe upon the congregation, perhaps in some measure owing to the silence of the night, particularly in singing the hymn with which we commonly conclude :

> Hearken to the solemn voice,
> The awful midnight cry !
> Waiting souls, rejoice, rejoice,
> And feel the Bridegroom nigh.

But London very soon ceased to be even the centre of Wesley's activities. In each place, where he had a congregation, beginning with Bristol, the faithful city, a room was provided, and the members were divided into classes " under the direction of those who could be trusted ". Each class was to meet weekly, and each member to help every other by opening their hearts in confession and their mouths in prayer. To this were added two practices which had in England the sanction of the Middle Age : itinerant missions and the preaching of men not in Holy Orders—both means of evangelisation resorted to, for a time at least, by the mendicant friars. Records of conversion from actively sinful or passively negligent lives produced men, whose hearts and souls were inspired by the mercy of God to preach the glad tidings of His salvation to men and women like themselves. The tales of these devoted helpers' lives are deeply touching : no mission to the heathen reveals more truly the turning of men from the power of Satan to God. And, under Him, it was the absolute sincerity and the glowing eloquence of Wesley which achieved this. The preaching of Tillotson (whose sermons were sold in large and repeated editions) and his school might teach wise men to be good and prudent men to be pious ; but (as was said of a nineteenth-century preacher) they could not convert a tomtit. Wesley's sermons came straight from his heart, as well as from his sound, strong head, and, if they did not stir the uneducated as did Whitefield's, they brought forth in abundance, among every class, the fruit of good living. For, in spite of the dangers inherent in his doctrine of assurance, there can be no doubt at all that Wesley, and his brother, and those who rightly followed in their ways, insisted upon the absolute necessity of personal holiness, of devotion to man, of sanctification to God.

The great work of Wesley undoubtedly was practical. There is much in his work, as in his character, which suggests comparison with a great statesman of the late nineteenth century. Like Mr. Gladstone, Wesley led men by his splendid eloquence and by the untarnished goodness of his personal life. But neither the one nor the other bequeathed to posterity literary work of permanent theological or political value. They spoke to their own time, and they spoke well; but posterity heeds rather their lives than their opinions. Yet Wesley, outside the realm of preaching, was keenly alive to the intellectual needs of his day. A passage in his letter to Middleton (regarded as a typical ' sceptic ' of his day) may illustrate this side of his activity :

"I have sometimes been almost inclined to believe ", he says, " that the wisdom of God has, in most later ages, permitted the external evidence of Christianity to be more or less clogged and encumbered for this very end, that men (of reflection especially) might not altogether rest there, but be constrained to look into themselves also, and attend to the light shining in their hearts. Nay, it seems (if it may be allowed to us to pry so far into the reasons of the divine dispensations) that, particularly in this age, God suffers all kinds of objections to be raised against the traditional evidence of Christianity, that men of understanding, though unwilling to give it up, yet, at the same time they defend this evidence, may not rest the whole strength of their cause thereon, but may seek a deeper and a firmer support for it. Without this I cannot but doubt whether they will long maintain their cause ; whether if they do not obey the loud call of God, and lay far more stress than they have hitherto done on this internal evidence of Christianity, they will not, one after another, give up the external, and (in heart at least) go over to those whom they are now contending with, so that in a century or two the people of England will be fairly divided into real Deists and real Christians. And I apprehend this would be no loss at all, but rather an advantage to the Christian cause. Nay, perhaps it would be the speediest, yea, the only effectual way of bringing all reasonable Deists to be Christians. . . . [Then to the Deists.] Go on, gentlemen, and prosper. Shame these nominal Christians out of that poor superstition which they call Christianity. Reason, rally, laugh them out of their dead empty forms, void of spirit, of faith, and love. . . . Press on, push your victories, till you have conquered all that know not God. And then He, whom neither they nor you know now, shall rise and gird Himself with strength, and go forth in His almighty love, and sweetly conquer you altogether." [1]

The passage ends with the practical note. That indeed was never absent. " I have one point in view," he said to Walker of Truro, " to promote, as far as I am able, vital, practical religion, and by the grace of God to beget, preserve, and increase the life of God in the souls of men."

It was not long after the definite establishment of Wesley's system, still in distinct adhesion to the Church of England, that his mother died on August 1, 1742. Her last

---

[1] Wesley's letter to Dr. Middleton, 1749. *Works*, x. 74-77.

days were passed " with no doubt or fear, nor any desire but, as soon as God should call, to depart and to be with Christ ". Already the son had become a prophet in his own country, for " an innumerable company of people " were gathered together when he committed her body to the ground. It was a time of sorrow, in other ways, to the sons. Not only was there the separation of friends, but the family, now sadly reduced in number from its original nineteen, had its tragic griefs. John's pupil at Lincoln, Westley Hall, had made love to his sister Kezia, promised to marry her—before her parents knew of the affair—and then jilted her to marry her sister Martha. Nor, it appears, was this the first change he had made in his affections within the Wesley family : he had before this courted Martha, and this was a return to his first love. But by no means his last. " It will not nor it cannot come to good," said wise Samuel of the marriage. And so it proved. Hall induced the discarded sister to live with his wife and himself. She soon died. He turned his wife out of doors. He became, in preaching and practice, a polygamist. Thirty years after his marriage he died, as Wesley believed, repentant. Hetty (Mehetabel), the liveliest of the daughters and the cleverest, after an early experience of sorrow, married a man quite unsuited to her, and lived but a few years after, " a gracious, tender, trembling soul " who found her consolation in the love of God. Another sister, Mary, married another pupil of John's, John Whitelamb, who became Vicar of Wroot, and is buried there. Theological disagreement intervened to mar the friendship with his old tutor. It may be that only by entire subservience was it possible to retain the entire affection of the great preacher. At Epworth there were not many memories of unbroken friendship. The village must have been, to all the Wesleys, charged with sad memories.

So it was that day when—Sunday, June 6, 1742—John, staying at the village inn, offered to help the curate, Mr. Romley, and was ungraciously refused. This is how he tells the tale in his *Journal* :

Sun. 6 June 1742. Epworth.—A little before the service began I went to Mr. Romley, the curate, and offered to assist him either by preaching or reading prayers ; but he did not care to accept of my assistance. The church was exceeding full in the afternoon, a rumour being spread that I was to preach. But the sermon on " Quench not the Spirit " was not suitable to the expectation of many of the hearers. Mr. Romley told them one of the most dangerous ways of quenching the Spirit was by enthusiasm ; and enlarged on the character of an enthusiast in a very florid and oratorical manner. After sermon John Taylor stood in the churchyard, and gave notice, as the people were coming out, " Mr. Wesley, not being permitted to preach in the church, designs to preach here at six o'clock ". Accordingly at six I came, and found such a congregation as I believe Epworth never saw before. I stood near the east end of the church, upon my father's tombstone, and cried, " The Kingdom of Heaven is not meat and drink ; but righteousness and peace and joy in the Holy Ghost ".

It was a wonderful scene : one of the most moving in the history of the Church. For a whole week he preached daily on the same spot; and the friends of his youth, the children his father and himself had christened, the neighbours who had heard of all he had done afar off, heard in wonder and thankfulness. Among them was Whitelamb. The pupil's offer of help, mingled with criticism, was not refused, but Wesley was called to other duties. The memory of that week was never forgotten : a memory charged with sorrow, which yet God turned to joy. And the pathos and tragedy were increased a year later when the curate actually refused the communion to the great Evangelist. Wesley's comment in his *Journal* speaks to the heart : [1]

" How wise a God ", says he, " is our God ! There could not have been so *fit* a place under

---

[1] Southey, vol. i. p. 320.

heaven, where *this* should befall me : first, as my father's house, the place of my nativity, and the very place, where *according to the strictest sect of our religion*, I had so long *lived a Pharisee*. It was also *fit*, in the highest degree, that he who repelled me from that very table, where I had myself so often distributed the bread of life, should be one who owed his all in this world to the tender love which *my* father had shown to *his*, as well as personally to himself."

Wesley was now embarked on a life of constant journeying, which he continued to the very end. And he noted its details in his *Journal* with an exactness which makes that extraordinary record a mine of interest. His letters, and the anecdotes of him, fill up the wondrous tale. He and his brother and their followers were accused of being Jacobites in the dangerous days of the '45, and he was even brought before magistrates because he had prayed that God would cause His banished ones to return : the magistrates were men of common sense and dismissed the charge.

Bishop Lavington's *The Enthusiasm of Methodists and Papists Compared* (second edition, 1749) is a curious illustration of feeling which was not at all uncommon in his time. The Methodists are " a dangerous and presumptuous sect, guilty of extravagant freaks ", and the author cautions all Protestants by his " comparison between the wild

G

and pernicious enthusiasm of some of the most eminent saints in the Popish communion and those of the Methodists in our own country ". It is a curious comparison : Wesley is found to have the same experiences as S. Francis, S. Ignatius, and S. Dominic : the inference to-day might be different. The comparisons are minute and often quite accurate : the animus is obvious, and the conclusions drawn might well reflect on every form of genuine religion, revealed or experienced. But, on the other hand, points are acutely observed in which the Methodists were really open to the criticism of sincere and thoughtful men. What a bishop could argue seriously, uneducated people could regard as certain : Wesley was a Papist, a traitor, and that with no necessity on the part of his accuser to produce any evidence—" All the gentlemen in those parts say that you have been a long time in France and Spain, and are now set hither by the Pretender and that these societies are to join him ". He was mobbed as a Jesuit. He was attacked as a Dissenter. Every abusive term that could be found was flung at him. He was often in danger of his life. But still he went everywhere and did everything. He avoided neither the rich nor the poor. At home with the miners of Kingswood and the fishermen of Whitby, he was equally prepared to cope with the fashionable of Bath and the egregious Beau Nash. Nash seems to have interrupted one of his discourses by asking by what authority he preached— that was easily answered out of the Ordination of Priests—and telling him that his preaching frightened people out of their wits. He admitted that he had never heard him but spoke from common report. " Sir," said Wesley, " is not your name Nash ? I dare not judge of you by common report : I think it not enough to judge by." This was at the beginning of Wesley's fame. Five-and-twenty years later he says of another visit to Bath, the date is Sunday, the 5th June 1766 : [1]

Oct. 5. Sun. At eight I administered the Sacrament at Lady Huntingdon's Chapel in Bath. At eleven I preached there on those words in the gospel for the day, " Thou shalt love thy neighbour as thyself ". The word was quick and powerful ; and I trust many, even of the rich and great, felt themselves sinners before God.

It is recorded that :

the Chapel was attended by not a few of the nobility : as Lord Camden, Lord Chancellor of England, Lord Northington, Earl Chatham and family, Lord Rockingham, Lady Malpas, Lord and Lady Powys, Lord and Lady Buchan, the Duke of Bedford and family, Dr. Barnard, Bishop of Londonderry.

[1] *Journal*, vol. v. p. 188, 1766.

Horace Walpole was there at the time and wrote to John Chute on October 10, 1766 :

I have been at one opera—Mr. Wesley's. They have boys and girls with charming voices ; that sing hymns in parts to Scotch ballad tunes ; but, indeed, so long that one would think they were already in eternity, and knew not how much time they had before them. . . . Wesley is a clean, elderly man, fresh-coloured, his hair smoothly combed, but with a little soupçon of curl at the ends. Wondrous clever, but as evidently an actor as Garrick. He spoke his sermon, but so fast, and with so little accent, that I am sure he has often uttered it, for it was like a lesson. There were parts and eloquence in it ; but towards the end, he exalted his voice, and acted very ugly enthusiasm, decried learning, and told stories like Latimer, of the fool of his college, who said, " I *thanks* God for everything ". Except a few from curiosity, and some *honourable women*, the congregation was very mean.

Later on Bath in his *Journal* has another mention, of half-admiring solemnity :

Wed. 3 [March 1790]. I took a view of the new buildings. There are at present none like them in England. They have not only added a second crescent, with two beautiful rows of houses near Lansdown, but a whole town on the other side of the city, which is swiftly increasing every day. And must all these fine buildings be burnt up ? Yea—" Earth and Heaven destroyed, nor left even one in the mighty void."

Such reflections were very common in

Wesley's thoughts.   He constantly dwelt on the disappearance of the present, particularly material things, buildings or outward shows and pomp.   He had no artistic taste, nor any sympathy for connoisseurs.

Horace Walpole had described Lady Huntingdon's chapel thus :

The chapel is very neat, with true Gothic windows. Yet I am not converted, but I was glad to see luxury creeping in upon them before persecution ; they have very neat mahogany for branches and brackets of the same taste.   At the upper end is a broad *haut pas* of four steps advancing in the middle ; at each of the broadest parts are two of my eagles, with red cushions for the parson and clerk.   Behind them rise three more steps, in the middle of which is a third eagle for pulpit.   Scarlet arm chairs for all three.   On either hand a balcony for elect ladies.   The rest of the congregation sit on forms.   Behind the pit in a dark niche, is a plain table within rails ; so you see the *throne* is for the *apostle*.

The chapel is not very much changed to-day.   The three eagles are there still : each has a monogram, which at first one supposes to be the Christian I H S.   But it is nothing so idolatrous : two are S.H., one T.H., for the countess and her husband.   One may now suspect where was " Nicodemus corner " where bishops used to sit concealed lest they should be thought to favour Enthusiasm. Then, as often, *episcopi Anglicani semper pavidi*. The chapel stands at the back of what was Lady Huntingdon's house in the Vineyards, and the gallery facing the preacher has an organ in it and was approached, after the fashion in country houses, directly from the first floor of the mansion itself.

There was no mobbing at Bath ; but in very many places there was. The discreditable record need not be enlarged upon. Mob violence, as the Gordon Riots showed, was in the eighteenth century at its height. The magistracy was not at its best for wisdom or impartiality, nor the clergy for their learning or charity. The preaching of morals without theology had not converted England to wisdom or goodness. But the law when it was enforced soon put things straight : soon it was enforced ; and the last years of Wesley's preaching were for the most part undisturbed in respect and honour. The opposition he received was now literary rather than physical ; and that quite naturally continued to the end.

# CHAPTER V

## THE WORK OF THE PREACHER

WESLEY'S work was pre-eminently practical; and everything else, or almost everything, he felt, must be sacrificed to the great task of drawing men, by whatever way, but chiefly by the words of love, to God. Already critics began to say that the methods were contrary to those of the Church of England : they said it before of reformers : they have said it since : they say it still. His method of work meant schism, they declared. Did it ? Southey says very happily :

Schism, according to Wesley, has almost always been wrongly defined a separation *from* a Church, instead of a separation in a Church. Upon his own definition, he himself was more peculiarly guilty of the offence : and however much he contended against those of his followers who were for separating from the Establishment, it is scarcely possible that he should not have foreseen the separation to which all his measures tended. Those measures were taken in good faith, and with good intent ; most of them indeed arising, unavoidably, from the circumstances in which he found himself ; but this was their direct, obvious, inevitable tendency. One step drew on another. Because he preached an enthusiastic and dangerous doctrine, which threw his hearers into convulsions, he was properly, by most clergymen, refused the use of their pulpits. This drove him to field-preaching : but field-preaching is not for all weathers, in a climate like ours. Prayer-meetings also were a part of his plan : and thus it became expedient to build meeting-houses. Meeting-houses required funds ; they required ministers too, while he was itinerating. Few clergymen could be found to co-operate with him ; and though at first he abhorred the thought of admitting uneducated laymen to the ministry, lay preachers were soon forced upon him, by their own zeal, which was too strong to be restrained, and by the plain necessity of the case.[1]

The history of his lay preachers is a chequered one. Some were very good men ; some were educated men ; some were very much the reverse of either. That he was obliged to employ some who were unworthy was really due to the overwhelming demands of his work. The people were crying for bread, and it seemed to him that the parochial clergy were giving them a stone ; yet when they asked for a fish he himself sometimes unconsciously gave them a serpent. And the serpent sometimes turned and bit him.

Originally the lay preachers lived, as did

[1] *Life*, i. 283.

the friars, on alms ; but Wesley soon under-
took to procure them salaries, and he en-
thusiastically set to work to see that their
children were educated. For this purpose
he established a school at Kingswood, three
miles from Bristol. Nothing shows better
his determination and his weakness. He
really did not know at all how to treat
children, and he thought he knew everything. Southey's description of the school
is entirely just.[1]

The children were to rise at four, winter and
summer ; this Wesley said he knew, by constant
observation and by long experience, to be of admirable use, either for preserving a good or improving a bad constitution ; and he affirmed that
it was of peculiar service in almost all nervous
complaints, both in preventing and in removing
them. They were to spend the time till five in
private, partly in reading, partly in singing, partly
in prayer, and in self-examination and meditation,
those that were capable of it. Poor boys ! they
had better have spent it in sleep. From five till
seven they breakfasted and walked, or worked, the
master being with them ; for the master was constantly to be present ; and there were no holidays,
and no play, on any day. Wesley had learnt a sour
German proverb, saying, " He that plays when he
is a child, will play when he is a man " ; and he
had forgotten an English one, proceeding from good
nature and good sense, which tells us by what kind
of discipline Jack may be made a dull boy. " Why ",

[1] *Life*, ii. 523.

he asks, " should he learn, now, what he must unlearn by and by ? " Why ? for the same reason that he is fed with milk when a suckling, because it is the food convenient for him. They were to work in fair weather, according to their strength, in the garden ; on rainy days, in the house, always in the presence of a master ; for they were never, day or night, to be alone. This part of his system Wesley adopted from the great school at Jena, in Saxony : it is the practice of Catholic schools, and may, perhaps, upon a comparison of evils, be better than the opposite extreme, which leaves the boys, during the greater part of their time, wholly without superintendence. At a great expense of instinct and enjoyment, and of that freedom of character, without which the best character can only obtain from us a cold esteem, it gets rid of much vice, much cruelty, and much unhappiness. The school-hours were from seven to eleven, and from one to five : eight was the hour for going to bed : they slept in one dormitory, each in a separate bed : a master lay in the same room, and a lamp was kept burning there. Their food was as simple as possible, and two days in the week no meat was allowed.

One of the lessons, or diversions, was to take the children to see a corpse ; and the poor little creatures were encouraged to conversion, which can hardly have avoided hysteria, or to stony callousness, still more grievous to Wesley. Writing in his *Journal* [1] on May 5, 1768, he says : " About this time a remarkable work of God broke out among

[1] Vol. v. pp. 248, 899.

the children at Kingswood School. One of the masters sent me a short account of it as follows :

*April* 27, 1768.

REV. AND DEAR SIR—On Wednesday the 20th God broke in upon our boys in a surprising manner. A serious concern had been observable in some of them for some time past ; but that night, when they were in their private apartments, the power of God came upon them, even like a mighty, rushing wind, which made them cry aloud for mercy. Last night, I hope, will never be forgotten, when about twenty were in the utmost distress. But God quickly spoke peace to two of them, J[ohn] G[lascot], and T[homas] M[aurice]. A greater display of His love I never saw ; they did indeed rejoice with joy unspeakable. For my own part, I have not often felt the like power. We have no need to exhort them to pray, for that spirit runs through the whole school : so that this house may well be called ' an house of prayer '. While I am writing, the cries of the boys, from their several apartments, are sounding in my ears. There are many, still lying at the pool, who wait every moment to be put in. They are come to this, ' Lord, I will not, I cannot, rest without Thy love '. Since I began to write, eight more are set at liberty, and now rejoice in God their Saviour. The names of these are John Coward, John Lyon, John Maddern, John Boddily, John Thurgar, Charles Brown, William Higham, and Robert Hindmarsh. Their age is from eight to fourteen. There are but few who withstand the work ; nor is it likely they should do it long ; for the prayers of those that believe in Christ seem to carry all before them. Among the colliers likewise the work of God increases greatly ; two of the colliers' boys were justified this week. The number added to our society since the Conference is a hundred and thirty.

I had sealed my letter, but have opened it to inform you that two more of our children have found peace. Several others are under deep con- viction. Some of our friends from Bristol are here, who are thunderstruck. This is the day we have wished for so long : the day you have had in view, which has made you go through so much opposition for the good of these poor children.

JAMES HINDMARSH."

To this amazing letter are added two more brief notes, ending with " the Lord is still with them, though not so powerfully as He was two or three weeks since ".

Had not Wesley so obviously approved, one might be disposed to set this dreadful record down to the ignorant enthusiasm of a diseased brain ; but Wesley was clearly satis- fied that this was a " remarkable work of God ''. The boys, Mr. Hindmarsh (who became a Swedenborgian preacher) thought, were "justified". Was he ; or was John Wesley ? After the visit to the corpse, the scene that occurred, says Southey, was worthy of Bedlam. It is hard to understand how good men can ever have believed that God works in such a way upon the souls of little children. It is strange that Wesley should ever have believed the school to be a success.

Too much indeed depended on Wesley ; and too much did he take upon himself. His masterful genius almost always carried him through. His labours were stupendous : no wonder that his judgement was not always sound, for the physical strain that he continually placed upon himself must have reacted unfavourably upon his mind. To give some idea of his enormous activities we must resort to his *Journal*. A few extracts, taken almost at random, will best illustrate the strength of his character and the nobleness of his Evangelistic work. Let us begin with one, most characteristic, which shows how little he envied or cared for, or perhaps even understood, the life of a country parson.

It was on November 5, 1766, I rode by Shoreham to Sevenoaks. In the little journeys which I have lately taken, I have thought much on the huge encomiums which have been for many ages bestowed on a *country life*. How have all the learned world cried out—" O fortunati nimium, sua si bona norint Agricolae ! " But, after all, what a flat contradiction is this to universal experience ! See that little house, under the wood, by the river-side ! There is rural life in perfection. How happy, then, is the farmer that lives there ! Let us take a detail of his happiness. He rises with, or before the sun, calls his servants, looks to his swine and cows, then to his stables and barns. He sees to the ploughing and sowing his ground, in winter or in spring. In summer and autumn he hurries and sweats among his mowers and reapers. And where is his happiness in the meantime ? Which of these employments do we envy ? or do we envy the delicate repast that succeeds, which the poet so languishes for ?

O quando faba, Pythagorae cognata, simulque
Uncta satis pingui ponentur oluscula lardo ?

Oh the happiness of eating *beans well greased with fat bacon* ! Nay, and *cabbage* too ! Was Horace in his senses when he talked thus, or the servile herd of his imitators ? Our eyes and ears may convince us there is not a less happy body of men in all England than the country farmers. In general, their life is supremely dull : and it is usually unhappy too. For, of all people in the Kingdom, they are most discontented ; seldom satisfied either with God or man.[1]

The fascination of his *Journal* is well illustrated by this extract. It lies in the writer's keenness of observation. He seemed to see everything, and note everything : character, scenery (sometimes), architecture, incidents of humour and pathos ; all seen from a spiritual standing-point. No doubt a great part of his charm lay in his overflowing humanity. Here is another passage from the same year : [2]

. I took a view of Beverley Minster, such a parish Church as has scarce its fellow in England. It is a most beautiful as well as stately building, both within and without, and is kept more nicely clean than any cathedral which I have seen in the King-

[1] *Journal*, vol. v. p. 191.
[2] Vol. v. p. 110. Saturday, 19 July 1766.

dom : but where will it be when the earth is burned up, and the elements melt with fervent heat ? About one I preached at Pocklington (though my strength was much exhausted), and in the evening at York.

It has been very well said that Wesley's " journal of missionary travel would serve as a guide-book to the British Isles, and is replete with romantic incident and graphic pictures of life and manners ".[1]

His work was far from confined to England. When he was seventy-nine he went to Holland. From almost the beginning of his Evangelistic career he visited Scotland, and from 1747 he paid constant visits to Ireland. He held a conference at Limerick in 1752. Dr. Curnock in his classic edition of the *Journal* [2] gives an admirable summary of Methodism outside England. He says :

The reception Methodism met with in Ireland is an interesting study. Across the Tweed it might seem to have comparatively failed. Scotland did not approve Arminian doctrine or Methodist itinerancy. A wider outlook leads, however, to an opposite conclusion. In no part of the empire was its success more remarkable ; but it differed in character. It did for the Church in Scotland that which Wesley hoped for in the Church of England : it leavened the three measures of meal, on the testimony of impartial witnesses, " until

---

[1] *Dict. Nat. Biog.* [Dr. A. Gordon].
[2] Vol. v. p. 126.

the whole was leavened ". It never attacked Pres-
byterianism, but, treating it with high courtesy,
eventually kindled its coldness into fire. One of
the earliest and most striking results was seen in
America, where Scotch and Irish Presbyterians
hailed Irish and English Methodists as spiritual
kinsmen and created the " Camp-Meeting ".[1] In
Scotland itself " the movement . . . became to a
considerable extent a religious movement ' within '
the Scottish Church ".[2]

In Ireland Methodism might in like manner
have leavened the Catholic population, whether
Roman or Anglican, and would have done so
but for the " non possumus " of Rome and the
short-sightedness and ferocious bigotry of certain
English Protestants. Wesley and his preachers
frequently won favour with the Papists, as almost
invariably with soldiers, sailors, children, and all
persons, scholarly or unsophisticated, of a childlike
spirit. If we except a few abnormal outbreaks,
accounted for by special indictments, Wesley was
almost as immune from persecution in Ireland as
in Scotland. Dublin and Aberdeen treated him
first with wondering and then with profound respect.
To both countries he was indebted for helpers,
men and women of a singularly high order. The
difference—and there was, and is, a very real
difference—between Scotch and Irish Methodism
may be illustrated by our Lord's twin parables.
If in Scotland the new presentation of the kingdom
of heaven was as leaven hidden, in Ireland it was
the grain of mustard-seed planted.

That is the view of modern Methodism.
But Wesley himself never showed real sym-

[1] Briggs, *Life of Asbury*, pp. 315-317.
[2] Butler's *Wesley and Whitefield in Scotland*, preface and
pp. 216-230.

pathy with the Presbyterian form of worship. He wrote on Sunday, May 10, 1772 :

> I attended the Church of England service in the morning, and that of the Kirk in the afternoon. Truly " no man having drunk old wine straightway desireth new ". How dull and dry did the latter appear to me, who had been accustomed to the former.[1]

But several passages in the *Journal*, notably in 1766, show him as much interested in Scottish as in English religion. Thus :

> Wed. 18. I set out for Glasgow.[2] In the afternoon the rain poured down, so that we were glad to take shelter in a little house where I soon began to talk with our host's daughter, eighteen or nineteen years old. But to my surprise, I found her as ignorant of the nature of religion as a Hottentot. And many such have I found in Scotland ; able to read, nay, and repeat the Catechism, but wholly unacquainted with true religion, yea, and all genuine morality. This evening we were in the house, but the next I preached abroad to many more than the house could contain. On *Friday* the number was greatly increased, but much more on *Saturday*. I then enlarged upon communion with God, as the only real, scriptural religion ; and I believe many felt that, with all their orthodoxy, they had no religion still.

And again, five days later, Monday, June 23, 1766 : [3]

> We rode in a mild, cool day to Thornhill, about sixty (measured) miles from Glasgow. Here I met

[1] Vol. v. p. 459.    [2] Vol. v. p. 170.    [3] Vol. v. p. 171.

H

with Mr. Knox's *History of the Church of Scotland*; and could any man wonder if the members of it were more fierce, sour, and bitter of spirit than some of them are ? For what a pattern have they before them ! I know it is commonly said, " The work to be done needed such a spirit ". Not so ; the work of God does not, cannot need the work of the devil to forward it. And a calm, even spirit goes through rough work, far better than a furious one. Although, therefore, God did use, at the time of the Reformation, some sour, overbearing, passionate men, yet He did not use them *because* they were such, but *notwithstanding* they were so. And there is no doubt He would have used them much more had they been of a humbler and milder spirit.

And the next day (we are reminded of *Redgauntlet* : doubtless Scott had read the *Journal*) :

Tues. 24. Before eight, we reached Dumfries, and after a short bait pushed on in hopes of reaching Solway Firth before the sea was come in. Designing to call at an inn by the Firth side, we inquired the way, and were directed to leave the main road and go straight to the house which we saw before us. In ten minutes Duncan Wright was embogged. However, the horse plunged on, and got through. I was inclined to turn back ; but Duncan telling me I needed only go a little to the left, I did so, and sunk at once to my horse's shoulders. He sprung up twice, and twice sunk again, each time deeper than before. At the third plunge he threw me on one side, and we both made shift to scramble out. I was covered with fine, soft mud from my feet to the crown of my head ; yet, blessed be God, hurt not at all. But we could not cross till between seven and eight o'clock. An honest man crossed with us, who went two miles out of his way to guide us over the sands to Skinburness, where we found a little clean house, and passed a comfortable night.

Stories like this, of hardship and of delight in adventure, could be multiplied out of the eight thick volumes of the *Journal* almost *ad infinitum*. Perhaps the details of each year's work have now lost their interest : but the general impression cannot fade. Wesley's work was that of an evangelist primarily. Also he was an educationist, devoting himself to the production of cheap educational literature. He aspired even to be a physician, and his *Primitive Physick* (1747) was repeatedly re-published for a century—perhaps is even now : of course, it shows the usual arrogance of an amateur, for probably the only thing that stands out especially in its pages is a strong warning against the use of quinine (cinchona bark).

It is a mistake to consider that he ever fell under the ban of the Church. Some clergy undoubtedly regarded his work in their parishes as little better than poaching ; many thought his theology inadequate or erroneous. Some bishops—such as War-burton and Lavington—attacked him. Some

parish priests gladly welcomed him : some
bishops praised and blessed him.  In July
1776 he was at York, and after an early
sermon of his own he went to S. Saviours-
gate Church, and the rector observing him
during the prayers (for he was, as usual,
dressed in cassock, gown and bands) sent the
sexton to tell him that the pulpit was at his
service.  He preached on the gospel for the
day—" Not every one that saith unto Me,
Lord, Lord, shall enter into the Kingdom of
Heaven, but he that doeth the will of My
Father which is in Heaven ".  He says in
his *Journal*, " I did not see one person
laugh or smile, though we had an elegant
congregation ".

Why should they ? one says.  Because it
happened that this very rector had himself
warned his people against " that vagabond
Wesley ".  He had invited him that day
without knowing who he was, though probably almost every one else in the church
knew.  After the sermon the clerk told the
rector it was Wesley who had preached.
" We are trapped," said he, " but never
mind, we had a good sermon."  The Dean
of York (what business was it of his ?) re-
ported the rector to the Archbishop : but
the rector was beforehand with him, and Arch-

bishop Drummond said, " You did right ".
So before long rector and preacher repeated
the offence.  Not long after he preached in
Haworth Church, then famous as having had
Grimshaw as its parish priest, but before
many years the home of much more famous
personages.  Some of the rough folk whom
the Brontës knew must have listened to him
that day ;  and it is interesting that he noted
that there were many there " perverted by
the anabaptists ", and added, " I see clearer
and clearer none will keep to us, unless
they keep to the Church.  Whoever separates
from the Church will separate from the
Methodists."  He was still firm in his belief
that his work was entirely that of an ordained
minister of the English Church.  He still
urged Methodists to attend the services of
the Church, and that because the Methodist
service was, he says, " defective ".  And
defective it was, says his most accurate
biographer,[1] of set purpose, in order that
it might be supplemented by the stated
prayers of the Church.  But still there was,
and he knew it, a difficulty of reconciliation.
Some said the Methodists were already dissenters.

As Wesley reached the critical middle

[1] Tyerman, *Life of Wesley*, ii. 576.

period of life the question began more clearly
to arise : *quo tendis* ?  Whither would this
elaborate organisation, and this exclusion
from so many pulpits of the Church, the
animosity of so many of the clergy who
thought, as did their predecessors of the
Franciscans, that there was an unjustifiable
interference with their duties and their privileges, lead ?  Already men began to ask was
John Wesley at heart a Churchman or a
Dissenter ?  Modern biographers have given
different answers.  Dr. Simon, the most
recent, answers it, from the Wesleyan point of
view, in the same manner as did Dr. Overton
half a century ago, from the Churchman's
standing - point.  Both say that separation
was inevitable :  that Wesley's proceedings
really involved practical separation as well as
theoretical dissent.  That eminent Methodist the late Dr. Rigg went so far as to
declare that " the Society, as such, was in no
sense or degree any part of any dependency
of " the Church of England; and that " it
had no organic connection with it whatever ".
In this strange statement he must have forgotten that the original Methodists professed
to govern themselves entirely by the rules
of the Church.  And certainly we must not
forget  Wesley's  repeated  and  emphatic

declarations up to the very last that a Church of England man he was and so would live and die, and that no one who respected his wishes would ever separate from her. There are so many of these that the reader of his writings wearies of them. Dr. Simon's view would either convict Wesley of insincerity or decide that he did not know what he was doing. Either his truthfulness or his intellect seems to be impugned. But one need not hold either to have been at fault ; he was as impetuous and inconsistent as he was enthusiastic and sincere.

Wesley's attachment to the Church of England, inconsistent though his action constantly was, was no insincere or ignorant sentimentality. It was a reasoned attachment, such as made him observe Lent, use the mixed chalice, pray for the faithful departed, keep all festivals and fasts, enjoy cathedral music at the festivals, and rejoice when he could " have the Lord's Supper daily, a little emblem of the primitive Church ".

Some of these practices, though probably none of these opinions, he abandoned as the stress of life grew upon him. But, till old age, few of his inconsistences appeared. And at the period of his career which we have now reached there can be little or no doubt that

he was in intention entirely obedient to the
Church. If he disobeyed bishops, which it is
doubtful if he ever consciously did, it was with
the view that he was appealing from Philip
drunk to Philip sober, from an ill-informed
prelate to a godly and well-learned one.
Which did he consider the great Bishop
Butler? In August 1739 he had an interview
with him, after he had been prohibited from
preaching at Bristol. It is supposed [1] that
Butler may have given the order. When they
met, Butler, after Wesley had asked his advice,
said, "I will give it you freely. You have no
business here: you are not commissioned to
preach in this diocese; therefore I advise thee
to go hence." Did Wesley ever take advice
from his superiors? Not now certainly, for
he replied, "Being ordained as Fellow of a
College, I was not limited to any particular
cure, but have an indeterminate commission
to preach the word of God in any part
of the Church of England. I do not, therefore, conceive that, in preaching here, I break
any human law."

The full account of the interview was
printed by Hannah More, from Wesley's own
manuscript, which appears to have perished.
It is given in the standard edition of his

[1] See *Journal*, ii. 237.

*Journal*,[1] and very clearly shows Wesley's position at this time.

BISHOP. Why, sir, our faith itself is a good work ; it is a virtuous temper of mind.

MR. WESLEY. My lord, whatever faith is, our Church asserts we are justified by faith alone. But how it can be called a good work I see not : it is the gift of God, and a gift that presupposes nothing in us but sin and misery.

B. How, sir ! Then you make God a tyrannical Being if He justifies some without any goodness in them preceding, and does not justify all. If these are not justified on account of some moral goodness in them, why are those not justified too ?

W. Because, my lord, they " *resist His Spirit* "; because " they will not come to Him that they might have life " ; because they suffer Him not to " work in them both to will and to do ". They cannot be saved, because they will not believe.

B. Sir, what do you mean by faith ?

W. My lord, by justifying faith, I mean a conviction wrought in a man by the Holy Ghost, that Christ hath loved him, and given Himself for him, and that through Christ, his sins are forgiven. (The definition in the Homily.)

B. I believe some good men have this, but not all. But how do you prove this to be the justifying faith, taught by our Church ?

W. My lord, from her Homily on Salvation, where she describes it thus : " A sure trust and confidence, which a man hath in God that, through the merits of Christ, his sins are forgiven and he reconciled to the favour of God ".

B. Why, sir, this is quite another thing.

W. My lord, I conceive it to be the very same.

[1] ii. 256-257 *note*.

B. Mr. Wesley. I will deal plainly with you.
I once thought you and Mr. Whitefield well-meaning
men ; but I cannot think so now. For I have heard
more of you : matters of fact, sir. And Mr.
Whitefield says in his *Journal* : " There are promises
still to be fulfilled in me ". Sir, the pretending to
extraordinary revelations and gifts of the Holy
Ghost is a horrid thing—a very horrid thing !

W. My lord, for what Mr. Whitefield says, Mr.
Whitefield, and not I, is accountable. I pretend
to no extraordinary revelations or gifts of the Holy
Ghost : none but what every Christian may receive,
and ought to expect and pray for. But I do not
wonder your lordship has heard facts asserted
which, if true, would prove the contrary ; nor do
I wonder that your lordship, believing them true,
should alter the opinion you once had of me. A
quarter of an hour I spent with your lordship
before, and about an hour now ; and perhaps you
have never conversed one other hour with any one
who spake in my favour. But how many with
those who spake on the other side ? So that
your lordship could not but think as you do. But
pray, my lord, what are those facts you have
heard ?

B. I hear you administer the Sacrament in your
Societies.

W. My lord, I never did yet, and I believe
never shall.

B. I hear, too, that many people fall into fits in
your Societies, and that you pray over them.

W. I do so, my lord, when any show by strong
cries and tears that their soul is in deep anguish.
I frequently pray to God to deliver them from it,
and our prayer is often heard in that hour.

B. Very extraordinary, indeed ! Well, sir, since
you ask my advice, I will give it you very freely.
You have no business here ; you are not com-

missioned to preach in this diocese. Therefore I advise you to go hence.

W. My lord, my business on earth is to do what good I can. Wherever, therefore, I think I can do most good, there must I stay, so long as I think so. At present I think I can do most good here ; there-fore here I stay. As to my preaching here, a dis-pensation of the gospel is committed to me, and woe is me if I preach not the gospel wherever I am in the habitable world ! Your lordship knows, being ordained a priest, by the commission I then received I am a priest of the Church Universal. And being ordained as Fellow of a College, I was not limited to any particular cure, but have an indeterminate commission to preach the word of God in any part of the Church of England. I do not, therefore, conceive that, in preaching here by this commission, I break any human law. When I am convinced I do, then it will be time to ask, " Shall I obey God or man ? " But if I should be convinced, in the meanwhile, that I could advance the glory of God and the salvation of souls in any other place more than in Bristol, in that hour, by God's help, I will go hence, which till then I may not do.

It is a most striking interview, and each man speaks thoroughly in the character we know.

It does not appear that Butler and Wesley ever met again : but Wesley [1] read the *Analogy* and noted it as " a strong and well-wrote thesis ; but, I am afraid, far too deep for their understanding to whom it is primarily addressed ". This was in 1739. In 1768 he

[1] *Journal*, iii. 232.

read the book again and still thought it " too hard for most of those for whom it is intended. *Free thinkers*, so called, are seldom *close thinkers*. They will not be at the pains of reading such a book as this. One that would profit them must dilute his sense, or they will neither swallow nor digest it."

It is sad that Butler did not appreciate Wesley, and, indeed, gives us pause when we are in flow of eulogy upon the great evangelist, for of the wisdom of the bishop we can have no doubt. Was it the arrogance, the opinionated determination of Wesley, that made Butler warn him so seriously? It is impossible to doubt that there was reason for the warning, when we read again the stories of extravagant excitement, of hysteria, even madness, which marked some of the earlier missionary journeys. They form a strange contrast to the commonplace composure of ordinary eighteenth-century life ; and as the sermons and meetings of Methodism became common they gradually died down, though they have shown signs, even in recent years, of recrudescence. Butler, perhaps, did not see that they were not essential to the Wesleyan system. He knew human nature to the core : perhaps that is why he distrusted these worst expressions of its sub-conscious self.

Warburton, Bishop of Gloucester, was a personage very impressive in his own time, but quite unequal to the massive Butler. If Butler may have been expected to feel some sympathy with Wesley, Warburton never could be. He showed the climax of arrogance in his anti-Calvinism. He denounced " the fanatical idea of a *favoured elect*, which never existed but in over-heated brains, where reward and punishment are distributed, not on the proportion of merit and demerit, but on the diabolic dreams of certain eternal decrees of election and reputation, unrelated to any human principle of justice ".[1] Wesley might have been almost ready to agree with this, but there was at the root of his thought still a sort of subsidiary Calvinism ; and that Warburton detected at once and denounced. But more obviously than that he detested " enthusiasm ", a word which, till Wesley's life had changed its meaning, was always used in a bad sense. And Dr. Neville Figgis, who wittily said so many wise things, reminded us most truly [2] that " It is no bad thing if we could learn from a despised prelate of a day that is not ours, that good intentions alone are no sufficient guide to right action ;

---

[1] *Divine Legation*, iv. 423.
[2] *Typical English Churchmen*, Warburton, pp. 247-248.

and that the use of what intelligence we possess in order to learn the path of wisdom is no less a duty than the pursuit of the course which approves itself ". But, at the same time, it must not be forgotten that Bishop Warburton fully recognised the weakness of the Church of his day : he did not blame Wesley for trying to reform it but for the bad theology which he thought to be at the base of his work. " The Church," said he, " like the Ark of Noah, is worth saving, not for the sake of the unclean beasts and vermin that almost filled it, and probably made most noise and clamour in it, but for the little corner of rationality that was as much distressed by the stink within, as by the tempest without." [1]

In 1762 Warburton attacked Wesley in " The Doctrine of Grace, or the Office and Operations of the Holy Spirit vindicated from the Insults of Infidelity and the Abuses of Fanaticism ". It is a work of sharp criticism and heavy jocularity, thoroughly characteristic of the writer ; but it is something in favour of the overbearing prelate that he actually sent the work for Wesley to examine before he published it. Wesley replied tartly, it must be admitted. Whitefield joined in the

[1] *Letters to Hurd*, p. 114.

fray ; and many others too. Wesley thought he had "untwisted" Warburton's arguments. But the controversy continued with great satisfaction to the combatants for a considerable time without any one being one penny the worse. Certainly there could be no clergymen more unlike each other than Warburton and Wesley.

But while thus immersed in controversy and attacked on all sides Wesley had at least as many friends among the clergy as he had enemies. If Toplady called him " the most rancorous hater of the gospel system that ever appeared in this land ", moved " by Satanic shamelessness and Satanic guilt ", and Rowland Hill declared that he was " a venal profligate ", both " as unprincipled as a rook and as silly as a jackdaw ", Thomas Scott, Walker of Truro, Grimshaw of Haworth, Romaine, Venn, Perronet, Richard Cecil, and John Newton were proud to be his followers ; and so, most of all, was the holy Fletcher of Madeley, of whom Wesley wrote, " so blameless a character in every respect I have not found in England or America ". Whitefield, who had so sharply parted from him, when asked if he thought he should see him in Heaven, replied, " I fear not, for he will be so near the throne and we shall be

at such a distance that we shall hardly get
a sight of him ", and especially asked that
he would preach his funeral sermon. This
Wesley did, and repeated the sermon again
and again, to enormous crowds, at the end
of 1770.

During these years the great increase of
the professed members of the Methodist
Society caused much difficulty in supplying
to them the ministrations which they demanded. Even Wesley could not be everywhere at once ; Charles Wesley often hesitated to intrude where he did not know he
would be welcome ; and when the members
wished to receive the Holy Communion in
their own chapels, Wesley was not able to
compel them always to communicate in their
parish churches. For a time Maxfield, ordained in Ireland, acted for the Wesleys in
London when they were absent. But he
became one of the schismatics. Then Wesley,
still explicit in the need of episcopal ordination, heard of a certain Greek bishop in
England named Erasmus, and learnt from
the Bishop of Smyrna that he was Bishop of
Arcadia in Crete. He obtained, he says,
" abundant unexceptional credentials as to
his episcopal character ",[1] and caused John

---

[1] *Works*, x. 432.

Jones to be admitted to the order of deacon by the laying on of his hands. A certificate exists by which the same bishop declares that he admitted the Rev. Mr. W. C.[1] in 1764 to the order of the priesthood. The English bishops would not ordain Wesley's ministers; for the most part they thought them not qualified. The venomous Mr. Toplady published the information that this Greek bishop—and he regarded him as an impostor and a mendicant—had ordained deacons to help Wesley, and that Wesley had requested him to confer on himself the order of bishop. This is generally discredited, but is not perhaps impossible. Anyhow Wesley never claimed to have actually received Episcopal orders. But he gradually approached the opinion that it did not matter that he had not. He did, however, clearly state in 1788 that " men may call me a knave or a fool, a rascal, a scoundrel, and I am content, but they shall never by my consent call me a bishop ".[2] Steps were being taken in other bodies kindred to his own to create a new ministry. This was done in Lady Huntingdon's Connection. He himself said in 1780 that he had " as good a right to ordain as to administer the Lord's Supper ". The next

---

[1] Who was this ?   [2] *Works*, xiii. 71.

I

step was to give the Societies a fixed constitution.  This came, February 8, 1784, by
a " deed of declaration ", registered in the
Court of Chancery.  This marks a new and
definite advance.

# CHAPTER VI

## THE CONSTITUTION AND ITS WORKING

AT the beginning of 1784 Wesley was in London, not resting—for he never rested—but preparing in comparative quiet for a new journey. He was now eighty-one years of age, and some may think it charitable to suppose that his mental powers were beginning to be distorted or decayed. There were no outward signs of this, unless his acceptance of—what was to him—an entirely new theory of the ministry be accepted as such. He was still as busy with details as ever, and especially with urging on people the wisdom of early services : five o'clock indeed was a favourite time with him. He protested against the " impropriety of standing at prayer and sitting while giving praise ", a Presbyterian practice which it is to be feared that—as they sang a great deal—his people adopted from laziness. Physically he was as strong as ever. He went to Scotland, as far north as Elgin,

Aberdeen, and the miserable village of Keith.
He stayed with peers and such folk, but still
delighted in a meeting where he could see
" not a silk coat ".

Southwards through Newcastle he came
through the dales to Whitby, most beautiful
of eastern seaports, where the honest fisher
folk ever received him gladly.

> " The society here ", he wrote, " may be a
> pattern to all in England. They despise all orna-
> ments but good works with a meek and quiet
> spirit. I did not see a ruffle, no nor a fashionable
> cap, among them ; though many of them are in
> easy circumstances. . . . About forty had a clear
> witness of being saved from inward sin, and seemed
> to walk in the full light of God's countenance."

He went southward again and reached Epworth in time for his birthday. Thus he
wrote : [1]

> To-day I entered on my eighty-second year,
> and found myself just as strong to labour, and as
> fit for any exercise of body or mind, as I was forty
> years ago. I do not impute this to second causes,
> but to the Sovereign Lord of all. It is He who
> bids the sun of life stand still, so long as it pleaseth
> Him. I am as strong at eighty-one as I was at
> twenty-one ; but abundantly more healthy, being
> a stranger to the headache, toothache, and other
> bodily disorders which attended me in my youth.
> We can only say, " The Lord reigneth ! " While
> we live, let us live in Him. In the afternoon I

[1] *Journal*, vol. vi. p. 521, June 1784.

went to Gainsborough, and willingly accepted the offer of Mr. Dean's Chapel. The audience was large, and seemed much affected : possibly some good may be done even at Gainsborough.

A month later the annual Conference was held at Leeds. It was a momentous one. The original trust deed was accepted by which the property in the Methodist chapels was secured to the Wesleys, and there were now three hundred and fifty-nine of them. They were now more explicitly than before made the property of the Conference. In the deed, above mentioned, the names of the preachers who constitute the Conference are given, a Legal Hundred who became the governing body : it is declared that the majority shall be supreme ; but that no act shall be valid except forty members be present : that the Conference shall meet yearly for not less than five days or more than three weeks ; and that if it shall ever cease to meet, or be not validly continued, for three years it shall cease to exist : that it shall fill up vacancies and choose its own president and secretary, and may admit to or expel from the connection ; and that no one unless an ordained minister of the Church shall be admitted to the charge of a chapel for more than three years in succession.

When the members of the Conference

were put upon the list Wesley acted with his
usual arrogance, but it may well be with his
usual wisdom, in admitting to the Conference
only one hundred out of a hundred and
ninety-nine preachers. Wesley had to justify
his action—he never found the slightest difficulty in doing this—in a pamphlet entitled
" Thoughts upon some late occurrences "
(1785). But his thoughts were already turned
to another and a much wider question.

The Methodists of America had multiplied
exceedingly. Now that the War of Independence was over and the States were separated
from England, there was a national feeling
against the Church, which had always been
inadequately provided with priests, and was
now reduced to a very small fraction of those
whom it had possessed before the war. The
Methodists clamoured for the Sacraments, for
more ministers, for more definite supervision :
they appealed to John Wesley to come over
and help them.

There was no immediate answer, but this
was not long delayed. There is no doubt
that it was hurried to a decision not only by
the demands of America, but by the presence
of an ambitious and very well-spoken person,
Mr. Thomas Coke.

It is said that Wesley had long been con-

vinced that a priest had the right to ordain.
Questions arose—Did this right belong only
to one episcopally ordained ? Did it mean
also a power to consecrate a bishop ? Could
any priest consecrate a bishop ? But when
Wesley had made up his mind he never either
troubled himself about details or delayed to
put his own decision into practice.

On Wednesday, September 1, he wrote in
his *Journal* : [1]

Sept. 1, Wed. Being now clear in my own
mind, I took a step which I had long weighed in
my mind, and appointed Mr. Whatcoat and Mr.
Vasey to go and serve the desolate sheep in America.

Thur. 2. I added to them three more, which
I verily believe will be much to the glory of God.

It is an extraordinary thing that the name
of the person he made bishop is omitted :
though in the rough notes there occurs under
date of September 4 the words " Prayed :
ordained Dr. Coke ".

But the fact is clear enough, and its
intention too. Here is the certificate which
Wesley gave : [2]

To all to whom these Presents shall come.
John Wesley, late Fellow of *Lincoln* College in
*Oxford*, Presbyter of the Church of *England*, sendeth
with greeting. Whereas many of the People in

[1] Vol. vii. p. 15.
[2] From the *Journal*, vol. vii. p. 16, September 1784.

the Southern Provinces of *North America* who desire to continue under my care, and still adhere to the Doctrines and Discipline of the Church of *England*, are greatly distrest for want of ministers to administer the Sacraments of Baptism and the Lord's Supper according to the usage of the said Church. And whereas there does not appear to be any other way of supplying them with ministers. Know all men that I John Wesley think myself to be providentially called at this time to set apart some persons for the work of the ministry in *America*. And therefore under the Protection of Almighty God, and with a single eye to his glory, I have this day set apart, as a superintendent, by the imposition of my hands and prayer [being assisted by other ordained ministers], Thomas Coke, Doctor of Civil Law, a Presbyter of the Church of England, & man whom I judge to be well qualified for that great work. And I do hereby recommend him to all whom it may concern as a fit person to preside over the Flock of Christ. In testimony whereof I have hereunto set my hand and seal this second day of September in the year of our Lord one thousand seven hundred and eighty four.

JOHN WESLEY.[1]

Now it must be remembered that though he conferred upon him powers which he regarded as episcopal, Wesley always forbade Coke to call himself a bishop. Within a few months Coke and his coadjutors ordained Asbury, another minister of the Methodist Society; and other ordinations by Wesley

[1] Facsimile of Dr. Coke's ordination certificate. The original is preserved at the Wesleyan Mission House, London.

were—August 1, 1785, Pawson, Hanby, and
Taylor for Scotland ; in 1786, Keighley
and Atmore, also for Scotland, Warrener for
Antigua, and Hammet for Newfoundland.
Five more were set apart in 1787 ; two in 1788
for Scotland, and seven more in the same year,
with Alexander Mather as superintendent.
Finally, on February 27, 1789, Wesley, assisted
by two English priests, Dickenson and Creigh-
ton, set apart two more men as presbyters. In
1786 Wesley said : " Whatever is done in
America and Scotland is no separation from
the Church of England ".[1] But the latest of
these ordinations—and that in 1789 was the
last—were not given with this restriction.
Those ordained were regarded by Wesley
himself as his deputies, with the right to
minister the Sacraments, and to hand on their
rights to others.

In 1787 Wesley had had his chapels and
ministers licensed under the Toleration Act,
but still (he said) not as dissenters, but simply
" preachers of the Gospel ".

Thus, by the ordination of Coke, he at
last definitely cast off his old view, that which
is conveyed in the Ordinal of the Church of
England, that a bishop alone has power to con-
vey Holy Orders, that is, that the ministry of

[1] Tyerman, *Life of Wesley*, iii. 442.

the Church which had been in existence since
the Apostles' time should be continued and
reverently esteemed and conferred in the way
in which it always had been conferred.
It was a matter of principle, not of practice
merely. So the Church of England regarded
it. But so, now, did not Wesley. He would
clearly distinguish between the Church of
England, where are bishops with legal juris-
diction, and America, where there were no
bishops nor any parish ministers. It must
be said that, without doubt, Wesley was inconsistent. Southey [1] is not unjust when he says
that "Wesley's declared opinion respecting
the identity of the Episcopal and priestly
orders was contradicted by his own conduct ;
and it may be suspected that his opinion upon
the apostolical succession rested on no better
ground than its convenience to his immediate
purpose ". And the nature of the step taken
was speedily recognised. The Methodists
knew that it gave them freedom. The Church
knew that it meant separation. On both
these opinions Coke acted when he ordained
bishops for America. No doubt when Wesley
ordained Coke his intention was exactly as
Tyerman [2] describes it : " Wesley meant the
ceremony to be a mere formality, likely to

---

[1] *Life*, ii. 250.    [2] *Life of Wesley*, iii. 434.

recommend his delegate to the favour of the Methodists in America ; Coke, in his ambition, wished and intended it to be considered as an ordination to a bishopric ". But at the same time it must not be forgotten that Wesley was already fully persuaded in his own mind that " bishops and presbyters are one order ".[1]

Charles Wesley, not for the first time, looked askance at his brother's action, and the witty verse was no doubt written by him :

> How easy now are Bishops made
> At man or woman's whim ;
> Wesley his hands on Coke hath laid,
> But who laid hands on him ?

Indeed indirectly there was again a woman in the case : or at least behind the scenes. The imperious Countess of Huntingdon had long recognised her ministers as dissenting from the Church. The definitely Calvinistic Methodists could hardly be regarded as Church folk. But this, so long at least as Wesley lived, was never true of the English Methodists. Wesley repeatedly forbade his disciples to form a separate body or to leave the Church. And at the very end of his life he solemnly repeated his belief and his injunction : " I never had any design of

[1] *Journal*, iii. 229.

separating from the Church. I have no such design now. I do not believe the Methodists in general design it, when I am no more seen. I do, and will do, all that is in my power to prevent such an event. Nevertheless, in spite of all I can do, many of them will separate from it (though, I am apt to think, not one half, perhaps not one third of them). These will be so bold as to form a separate party, which, consequently, will dwindle away into a dry, dull, separate sect. In flat opposition to these, I declare once more that I live and die a member of the Church of England, and that none who regard my judgement will ever separate from it." Those last words remain as the solemn judgement of the greatest English evangelist of the eighteenth century.

But John Wesley was no prophet. This sect, when it was founded, did not decay but flourished and continues to flourish. It may be that all the consequences which he saw, and those which he did not foresee, would have never come to pass if only the English bishops had recognised more fully the mission of unlearned, or half-learned, men, and had admitted to Holy Orders many of the Methodist preachers. But again that was not all. Several of the preachers were " scholars and gentlemen ", but in very many cases their opinions were—to quote words of a bishop to-day—not only gravely divergent from, but also directly contrariant to, those of the English Church. However lightly the test was applied in those days, there was the theological barrier, and the bishops as a whole were determined to uphold it. And there, one can hardly doubt, Charles Wesley was of the same opinion as the bishops. He died in 1788. His loving heart could never allow a separation from the brother to whom he was devoted. But his judgement never varied. In 1785 he wrote of John :

I can scarcely yet believe it, that in his eighty-second year, my brother, my old intimate friend and companion, should have assumed the episcopal character, ordained elders, consecrated a bishop, and sent him to ordain our lay teachers in America. I was then in Bristol, at his elbow ; yet he never gave me the least hint of his intention. Lord Mansfield told me last year that ordination was separation. This my brother does not and will not see, or that he has acted contrary to all his declarations, protestations, and writings ; robbed his friends of their boasting, and left an indelible blot on his name so long as it shall be remembered.

This, it is not to be forgotten, is from one brother of another, from the founder of the Holy Club to the leader of the Methodists.

Dr. Watson, Regius Professor of Ecclesiastical History at Oxford, a candid and unprejudiced critic, has recently put the meaning of the separation with judicial lucidity.[1] He says that the whole tendency of Wesley's work

had been towards separation, and his teaching on the nature of the Church, combining as it did the doctrines of Hoadly and of Calvin, would furnish reasons to justify the measure which his followers were to take. For Wesley, churchman as he was, had been quite indifferent to churchmanship in the preachers whom he chose. Few of them had been attached members of the Church before they joined him ; many had been dissenters, and he had excited hostility among the dissenting bodies by enticing from them, as they regarded it, their hopeful recruits. But most of the preachers had been rescued from a careless life, and their first and only religious interest was in the Methodist Society. Whether they had been indifferent or dissenters they had no bond of affection to attach them to the Church of England, and it was inevitable that they should desire to make their Society complete in itself, administering its own sacraments as well as maintaining its own discipline.

Thus schism was inevitable, however little Wesley desired it. He desired to remain in the Church, but on his own terms. That, of course, was impossible. There was no strong body in the Church : Arminianism was still suspect : Calvinism was either

[1] *The Church of England*, p. 195.

hated or embraced with extravagant cordiality. Wesley was really devoted to the Church of which he was a minister, but in the rigid days wherein his lot was cast there was no permanent or consistent position for him in it, unless it were to make him its Pope. John Wesley was determined but he was inconsistent. Determination of character is an invariable necessity of greatness : consistency very rarely belongs to it.

# CHAPTER VII

## THE LAST YEARS

DURING all these years of theological strife and intellectual divergence or progress John Wesley continued his pastoral work, for the world which was his parish, with unremitting zest. His distant kinsman Arthur Wellesley might well have said of him, with more truth perhaps than of the British soldier, that he could go everywhere and do everything. A few more instances of his astounding activity may be given before the scene closes. But before that we may well turn to another side of his life, the scene of continual disappointment. It may be that domestic happiness is impossible for one of the temperament of John Wesley. At least he never attained to it. Even of his brother's affection he often seems almost impatient. Could he have made a happy marriage?

For several years after the unhappy result of his adventure with Sophia Hopkey Wesley was more careful in his relations with the fair sex. But it was impossible for young men so impressive and so popular to live without attracting the notice of the ladies who listened to them. Hutton, writing to Zinzendorf in 1740, said: "Both John Wesley and Charles are dangerous snares to many young women. Several are in love with them. I wish they were married to some good sisters, though I would not give them one of mine, even if I had many."[1] Ten years elapsed, and Charles married Sarah Griffith at Garth on April 8, 1749, and at that time John seemed likely very soon to follow his example.

In 1743, in a pamphlet on "Marriage and Celibacy", John Wesley had shown a preference, at least as regards an evangelist's work, for an unmarried life. The views of his Conference in 1748 appear to have caused him to alter his opinion. He had certainly thought much, and not impersonally, on the subject.

In his account of the earlier life Dr. John Simon says very truly:[2]

In the management of women Wesley often acted like an incurable optimist. He perceived in

---

[1] Benham, *Memoirs of James Hutton*, 46-47.
[2] *John Wesley and the Religious Societies*, p. 122.

K

them spiritual powers and intellectual graces un-
seen by less sympathetic observers. His misreading
of them stirred the wonder and the temper of his
brother Charles, and led to several regrettable
incidents. There is a touch of pathos in the
spectacle of John Wesley seated in the cabin of the
ship in which one of Oglethorpe's women servants
lay sick, reading to her long passages from the Cambridge Platonist's treatise on "Christian Prudence".
The maid recovered with startling rapidity.

The matter deserves a few words here, for
indeed everything that touches upon the
great preacher's relations with women is
worth investigation. Probably Wesley was
more foolish than philandering. He certainly did feel, as men of hurriedly active life
often do, the need of sympathy ; and in his
minor ailments he was greatly soothed by the
tenderness of women. But undoubtedly he
liked his women friends to be in subjection :
and that is where his own marriage came to
an unfortunate conclusion. This by the way,
for after all these incidents are quite in-
significant in proportion to the absorbing
interests of his evangelic life. Let us see
briefly what these episodes, these love affairs,
were.

The famous one, which has been described
in a clever book [1] as " John Wesley's Last
Love ", is that of Grace Murray. This

[1] By Prof. Leger of Brest.

young lady—Grace Norman—was born on January 18, 1716, was the child of Church folk, and serious (if intermittently) from her earliest years. In 1736 she married Alexander Murray, of a Scots Jacobite family, who had settled in England and become a sailor. During one of his absences she heard John Wesley preach, and found her " heart wholly drawn towards God ". She heard the preachers as often as she could and set herself to live as they wished and God ordained. When her husband returned he was angry at her persistence ; yet her gentleness won him at least to toleration, and they lived together happily till his next voyage, from which he never returned. From that time she became a regular member of the Society, a trusted class leader given to good works. She refused another marriage, and became an inmate of Wesley's household, practically a servant, though, as S. Paul would have said, a sister beloved by all who knew her piety and goodness. After the fashion of the time she kept a diary of her religious experiences : it is often, from its self-torture, painful reading. Of her practical goodness there was no doubt. To the sick whom Wesley often sheltered she was a ministering angel, and it was through nursing

John Bennet, one of Wesley's preachers, for six weeks, that she came to know him whom she eventually married. When John Wesley himself was ill she tended him too, and by the end of the year 1748 it was plain that he had fallen in love with her. She followed him in many of his journeys ; and at length he said, " We must part for a while : but if we meet again, I trust we shall part no more ". " It is impossible we should part," she said, " God has united us for ever."

Often, says Wesley, she repeated the assurance of her affection. On Sunday, September 17, 1749, he says, " We continued conversing together till late at night, and she gave me all the assurances which words could give of the most intense and inviolable affection. The same she renewed every day, yea, every hour when we were alone, unless when we were employed in prayer ; which indeed took up a considerable part of the time we spent together." It is a tangled tale. Charles set himself to prevent the marriage ; so did many who knew both the parties. Was she not already engaged to John Bennet ? Probably she was. She married him at Newcastle on October 3, 1749. For a time Wesley was heartbroken ; his *Journal*—and he did not hesitate to publish it later—was for a time full of bitter sorrow and bitter denunciations. He relieved his feelings by some very indifferent verses. He fasted and prayed, but " the sons of Zeruiah were too much for him ". He said, " The whole world fought against me ; but above all my own familiar friend ".[1] It is a sad tale. Years after, when both were grown old, they met, three years before Wesley's death : an affecting meeting, but " Mr. Wesley preserved more than his usual self-possession ". She lived into the nineteenth century.

There is no need to tell of the other ladies who loved the good man : indeed there were few who knew him that could help it. Surely among them he might have found a fitting bride. But it was not to be. His friend Vincent Perronet condoled with him on his disappointment, and urged him to try again. Many wondered that he did not marry Sarah Ryan, housekeeper at Kingswood, to whom he was the " affectionate ", and whom the lady he did marry referred to as having three husbands living, of different nationalities, in terms, says Dr. Gordon, " inelegant but exact ".

But he made another choice. Wesley's

---

[1] Wesley's *Works*, xiii. 163.

wide reading had no doubt made him familiar
with " Rule a wife and have a wife ". He
was to learn that it was difficult to rule but
quite easy to lose one.

In 1751 he determined that it was his
duty to marry. Again he astonished Charles
by his choice. It was through his brother
that John had come to know Mrs. Vazeille,
widow of a rich merchant. She was a
devotee, and, it seemed, a sincere as well as
a generous one. But the marriage was most
unhappy. The husband's autocratic temper
and his constant absence from his wife, and the
wife's irritability and suspicious nature, made
sincere affection impossible. Mrs. Vazeille
no doubt admired the great preacher, and
no doubt expected an increase of importance
for herself from being his wife. Wesley, it
seems probable, never really loved her : he
thought of her rather as a nurse and a housekeeper than as a wife. No need to tell the
story at length. Her jealousy and desire for
notoriety made her read his letters and
treacherously reveal his secrets. How he regarded this, and what sort of a husband he
must have been, is best seen in his very
characteristic letter of October 23, 1759.

DEAR MOLLY—I will tell you simply and plainly
the things which I dislike. If you remove them,

well. If not, I am but where I was. I dislike your showing any one of my letters and private papers without my leave. This never did any good yet, either to you, or me, or any one. It only sharpens and embitters your own spirit. And the same effect it naturally has upon others. The same it would have upon me but that (by the grace of God) I do not think of it. It can do no good. It can never bring me nearer, though it may drive me further off. And should you do as you often threaten me, then the matter is over. I know what I have to do. In all this you are fighting against yourself. You are frustrating your own purpose, if you want me to love you. You take just the wrong way. No one ever was forced to love another. It cannot be : love can only be won by softness ; foul means avail nothing. But you say, " I have tried fair means, and they did not succeed ". If they do not, none will. Then you have only to say, " This evil is of the Lord ; I am clay in His hand ".

I dislike (2) not having the command of my own house, not being at liberty to invite even my nearest relations so much as to drink a dish of tea without disobliging you. I dislike (3) the being myself a prisoner in my own house, the having my chamber door watched continually, so that no person can go in or out but such as have your good leave. I dislike (4) the being but a prisoner at large even when I go abroad, inasmuch as you are highly disgusted if I do not give you an account of every place I go to and every person with whom I converse. I dislike (5) the not being safe in my own house. My house is not my castle. I cannot call even my study, even my bureau, my own. They are liable to be plundered every day. You say, " I plunder you of nothing but papers ". I am not sure of that. How is it possible I should ? I miss money too, and he that will steal a pin will steal a pound.  But were it so, a scholar's papers are his treasure, my journal in particular.  " But I took only such papers as relate to Sarah Ryan and Sarah Crosby."  That is not true.  What are Mr. Landey's letters to them ?  Besides, you have taken parts of my journal which relate to neither one nor the other.  I dislike (6) your treatment of my servants (though, indeed, they are not properly mine).  You do all that in you lies to make their lives a burden to them.  You browbeat, harass, rate them like dogs, make them afraid to speak to me.  You treat them with such haughtiness, sternness, sourness, surliness, ill-nature, as never were known in any house of mine, for near a dozen years.  You forget even good breeding, and use such coarse language as befits none but a fishwife.

I dislike (7) your talking against me behind my back, and that every day and almost every hour of the day ;  making my faults (real or supposed) the standing topic of your conversation.  I dislike (8) your slandering me, laying to my charge things which you know are false.  Such are (to go but a few days back) that I beat you, which you told James Burges ;  that I rode in Kingswood with Sarah Ryan, which you told Sarah Rigby ;  and that I required you, when we were first married, never to sit in my presence without my leave, which you told Mrs. Lee, Mrs. Fry and several others, and stood to it before my face.  I dislike (9) your common custom of saying things not true.  To instance only in two or three particulars.  You told Mr. Ireland, " Mr. Vazzilla learnt Spanish in a fortnight ".  You told Mr. Fry, " Mrs. Ellison was the author as to my intrigue in Georgia ".  You told Mrs. Ellison, " You never said any such thing ; you never charged her with it ".  You also told her, " that I had laid a plot to serve you as

Susannah was served by the two elders ". I
dislike (10) your extreme immeasurable bitterness
to all who endeavour to defend my character (as
my brother, Joseph, Jones, Clayton Carthy), breaking
out even into foul, unmannerly language, such as
ought not to defile a gentlewoman's lips, if she did
not believe one word of the Bible.

And now, Molly, what would any one advise
you to that has a real concern for your happiness ?
Certainly (1) to show, read, touch those letters no
more, if you did not restore them to their proper
owner ; (2) to allow me the command of my own
house, with free leave to invite thither whom I
please ; (3) to allow me my liberty there, that any
one who will may come to me, without let or
hindrance ; (4) to let me go where I please, and to
whom I please, without giving an account to any ;
(5) to assure me, you will take no more of my
papers, nor anything of mine, without my consent ;
(6) to treat all the servants where you are (whether
you like them or no) with courtesy and humanity,
and to speak (if you speak at all) to them, as well
as others, with good-nature and good-manners ;
(7) to speak no evil of me behind my back ; (8)
never to accuse me falsely ; (9) to be extremely
cautious of saying anything that is not strictly
true, both as to the matter and manner ; and
(10) to avoid all bitterness of expression till you
can avoid all bitterness of spirit.

These are the advices which I now give you in
the fear of God, and in tender love to your soul.
Nor can I give you a stronger proof that I am your
affectionate husband.

It is a wonder, perhaps, that after this they
lived any longer together. The crudities and
cruelties of Mrs. Wesley's conduct are too

frequent for repetition. Some thought there were faults on both sides. Vincent Perronet [1] wrote to Charles Wesley in 1752 :

I think the unhappy lady is most to be pitied, though the gentleman's case is mournful enough. Their sufferings proceed from widely different causes. His are the visible chastisements of a loving Father; hers, the immediate effect of an angry, bitter spirit ; and indeed it is a sad consideration, that, after so many months have elapsed, the same warmth and bitterness should remain.

The most dreadful scene is that recorded by the preacher Hampson,[2] who said to his son :

I was once on the point of committing murder. Once, when I was in the North of Ireland, I went into a room, and found Mrs. Wesley foaming with fury. Her husband was on the floor, where she had been trailing him by the hair of his head ; and she was herself still holding in her hand venerable locks which she had plucked up by the roots. I felt as though I could have knocked the soul out of her.

This horrible woman often threatened to leave her husband, but often relented. He often forgave her, but as often returned to scolding and imperious love. She thought she had cause of jealousy : she did not understand his character. He could not trust her,

---

[1] Tyerman, ii. 108.        [2] Tyerman, ii. 110.

or bend her to his will.   At last comes the
entry in his *Journal*, January 23, 1771, that
she, " for what cause I know not, evidently
set out for Newcastle purposing ' never to
return '.   *Non eam reliqui : Non dimisi : Non
revocabo.*"

But these harsh words were not the last.
She was again with him for a time in 1772.
In 1777 at least he endeavoured to make a
reunion, but it must be on his own terms.
We do not know her reply.   On Friday,
October 12, 1781, occurs the entry : " I came
to London, and was informed that my wife
died on Monday.   This evening she was
buried, though I was not informed of it till
a day or two after."

So ended one of the bitter tragedies of
misunderstanding.   No doubt both had faults.
Hers were the more serious, if his might be
almost as hard to bear.   She had stolen his
letters, read them to his enemies, and allowed
them to misinterpret them.   She must, one
feels, often have been a little mad.   Was it
the rage of a woman not scorned, perhaps, but
often neglected ?   As to his feeling for others
of her sex certainly she never understood what
Alexander Knox   described with absolute
accuracy :   that it was his very nature " to
conceive such attachments, and the child-

like innocence of his heart disposed him to express them with the most amiable sincerity. The gaiety of his nature was so undiminished in its substance, while it was divinely disciplined in its movements, that, to the last hour of his life, there was nothing innocently pleasant with which he was not pleased, and nothing naturally lovely, which, in its due proportion, he was not ready to love." That, indeed, is the last word on the subject of Wesley's loves. How often good men have been maligned. How bitterly he must have suffered, how often concealed the wolf eating at his heart. But those who knew him trusted him and loved him. *Honi soit qui mal y pense.* And after the tragedy of his married life it is well to remember that in his wife's will, written three years after she left him, she bequeathed to him a mourning gold ring " in token that I die in love and friendship towards him ".

It is the fate, too often we sometimes feel, of those who have greatly helped others to live lonely lives, and to die, in a different sense from that in which Pascal speaks of death, alone. This did not happen to Wesley. As he came to great age he was surrounded by troops of friends. And—what there can be no doubt he more entirely rejoiced in—he

was able to work to the end. Not only that,
but he read to the end as well as wrote. In
his later years he only published, as he had
done for so long, the *Arminian Magazine*,
originally a counterblast against Calvinism,
now a straightforward expression of undisturbed faith. But he never ceased to read
" light literature ", or to express his generally
contemptuous opinion of it. Here is a passage
written when he was eighty-six : [1]

Mon. 28. I retired to Peckham, and at leisure
hours read part of a very pretty trifle—the *Life of
Mrs. Bellamy*. Surely, never did any, since John
Dryden, study more—" To make vice pleasing, and
damnation fine "—than this lively and elegant writer.
She has a fine imagination, a strong understanding,
an easy style, improved by much reading : a fine,
benevolent temper, and every qualification that
could consist with a total ignorance of God. But
God was not in all her thoughts. Abundance of
anecdotes she inserts, which may be true or false.
One of them concerning Mr. Garrick is curious.
She says : " When he was taking ship for England,
a lady presented him with a parcel, which she
desired him not to open till he was at sea. When
he did he found Wesley's hymns, which he immediately threw overboard." I cannot believe it.
I think Mr. Garrick had more sense. He knew my
brother well ; and he knew him to be not only far
superior in learning, but in poetry, to Mr. Thomson
and all his theatrical writers put together. None
of them can equal him, either in strong nervous
sense, or purity and elegance of language. The

musical compositions of his sons are not more excellent than the poetical ones of their father.

The great services of Samuel Wesley (1766–1837) have indeed added glory to the name. And his uncle John seems to have had some sense of this. He was truly a multifarious man. His interests were wide indeed. Notably, Wesley did not allow his religion to make him neglect the politics of his country. He was a keen observer of public events, a loyal subject, an even bitter opponent of those whose political principles did not suit his own. He was certainly no pacifist. He actually himself gathered troops for the service of the Crown. In 1756 it was that he actually raised a company of volunteers, and on March 1 he offered their services to the Government.[1] We do not know that any notice was taken of his offer. Governments do not think much of fighting parsons, or believe in their clerical drill. Even Charles Wesley laughed at his brother's soldiers.[2] John's loyalty was so great that he even " enlarged a little upon His Majesty's character ", while canvassing hard for Mr. Jarrit Smith in the Bristol election of 1756—a Tory

---

[1] See Simon, *Wesley and Advance of Methodism*, p. 317 ; cf. *Journal*, iv. 150-151.
[2] So says the standard edition of Wesley's *Journal*, vol. iv. p. 151 *note*.

whom George II. was supposed to favour. If Wesley was able to " enlarge " favourably upon the character of George II., one would expect him to speak well of George III. He does say in 1786 that he much doubts " whether there be any other king in Europe that is so great and natural a speaker ", but though in the political letter to Lord North [1] he describes himself as " a High Churchman, the son of a High Churchman, bred up from my child-hood in the highest notions of passive obedi-ence and non-resistance ", he writes very gingerly about the American War. He says nothing in praise of the King, and writes that in England, Scotland, and Ireland " the bulk of the people are ripe for rebellion : they want nothing but a leader ". Yet later on during the war he seemed to side against the colonists. The titles of two pamphlets of 1775 show the criticisms to which he exposed himself. They are " A Letter to the Rev. John Wesley, occasioned by his calm Address to the American Colonies ", by " Ameri-canus ", 1775 ; and " An Old Fox Tarr'd and Feathered, occasioned by what is called Mr. John Wesley's Calm Address to our American Colonies ", by " Hanoverian ". The " Old Fox " was accused of blowing hot and

---

[1] Wesley's *Journal*, standard edition, viii. 325.

cold from the same mouth, and still more
bitterly of plagiarising Dr. Johnson's much
more famous pamphlet—the latter charge one
which would certainly leave Wesley cold, for,
like Molière, unblushingly he took what he
thought good wherever he found it.

One could think the conclusion to be that
he was very like most clergymen : he knew
very little indeed about politics or war, but
thought he knew a great deal ; and did not
hesitate to express his opinions vociferously,
but with inadequate knowledge.   An opinion
he expresses after a debate among the Peers
is eminently characteristic : [1]

Tues. 25 [January 1785].   I spent two or three
hours in the House of Lords.   I had frequently
heard that this was the most venerable assembly in
England.   But how was I disappointed ! What is
a lord but a sinner, born to die !

His political pamphlets, it must be admitted, are not of great value.   Yet in his
intense social interests combined with conservative instincts he may be regarded as the
forerunner of many later Conservative politicians, and " Tory democrats ", whose influence is indeed now stronger than ever.
Many of his apophthegms illustrate this position.   " Christianity", he said, " is a social

[1] *Journal*, vol. vii. p. 46.

religion : and to turn it into a solitary one is
to destroy it " ; [1] and so " there is the closest
connection between my religion and my political conduct ", and " the self-same authority
enjoins me to ' fear God ' and to ' honour the
King ' ", he wrote on June 25, 1777. If he
ceased to be, in the old sense, a Church man
he never ceased to be a King's man.

With him religion and philanthropy were
the keystone of politics : that is the thought
which underlies all his political writings ;
and in nothing is it better illustrated than in
his protests against slavery. The last letter
he wrote was to Wilberforce. It was dated
a week before his death, and thus it runs :

MY DEAR SIR—Unless the Divine Power has
raised you up to be as Athanasius *contra mundum*,
I see not how you can go through your glorious
enterprise in opposing that execrable villainy which
is the scandal of religion, of England, and of human
nature. Unless God has raised you up for this
very thing, you will be worn out by the opposition
of men and devils ; *but if God be for you, who can
be against you ?* Are all of them stronger than God ?
Oh, " be not weary in well-doing ". Go on, in
the name of God and in the power of His might,
till even American slavery, the vilest that ever saw
the sun, shall vanish away before it.

Reading, this morning, a tract, written by a poor
African, I was particularly struck by that circum-
stance—that a man who has a black skin, being

------

[1] *Works*, v. 297.

L

wronged or outraged by a white man, can have no redress : it being a *law*, in our colonies, that the *oath* of a black, against a white, goes for nothing. What villainy is this ?

That He who guided you, from your youth up, may continue to strengthen you in this and all things, is the prayer of, dear sir, your affectionate servant,                                JOHN WESLEY.

After the act which his brother Charles and the great lawyer Mansfield regarded as involving separation, John Wesley continued his itinerant work with but little sign of failing strength. It has been estimated that during the course of his life he travelled two hundred and fifty thousand miles and preached forty thousand sermons. It is not to be wondered at that his sermons [1] do not often reach the highest standard. They compare, when they are read in cold daylight, with the speeches of Mr. Gladstone, whom in character the preacher in many respects resembled. The effect of each when they were delivered was extraordinary : instructive, convincing, converting, are words which their hearers must often have applied to them. And even when read to-day, when taste has changed so completely, Wesley's appeals have often a most impressive force. They are so obviously sincere, so heartfelt ; so plainly

---

[1] Two vols., London, 1825.

are they full of the love of God and the love of man. They show an intimate knowledge of human nature, perhaps more often on its dark than on its bright side, and a knowledge, most intimate, of temptation, varied and seductive. Indeed, when one reads them again, it is very difficult to criticise them. At first, it may have been felt : they are too long : and they are artificial. But, as for length, the people hung on his words, they loved to have it so : if the hour-glass had still been in fashion his hearers would often have begged him to turn it. And as for artifice, Wesley certainly knew how to win over a crowd, how to arrest attention and to retain it : yet very likely he would have said, " Sir, I swear I use no art at all ", if one had questioned him ; for always, one feels certain, he spoke from his heart. Let us stay our judgement so. It is impossible to feel that his sermons have quite the beauty or the simplicity of Newman's ; yet it may well be when we feel impatient of them that it is weakness of character, our reluctance to hear the full truth, that makes us critical. The theology, we may often feel, and perhaps justly, is sometimes harsh, often inadequate ; but the moral touch is almost invariably sure. We could not find a better motto, let us say, for the whole of them, a more genuine summary of the thought which lies behind every one, than the fine words in *An Earnest Appeal*.[1]

We see (and who does not ?) the numberless follies and misdeeds of our fellow creatures. We see, on every side, men of no religion at all, or men of a lifeless, formal religion. We are grieved at the sight ; and should greatly rejoice, if by any means we might convince some that there is a better religion to be attained—a religion worthy of God that gave it. And this we conceive to be no other than love : the love of God and of all mankind ; the loving God with all our heart, and soul, and strength, as having first loved *us*, as the fountain of all the good we have received and of all we ever hope to enjoy ; and the loving every soul which God hath made, every man on earth, as our own soul.

Preaching animated by this spirit continued to the end of Wesley's life. This was now drawing nigh. During the last year of his life he was much in the east and the north. One of the places, it seems, that Wesley most loved, was Whitby, the wonderful old town which creeps up the hillside to the church, and the ruined abbey at the top. The church to-day is very much what it was in the eighteenth century : a fine Norman building—and more Norman work, long forgotten, has recently been revealed—changed

[1] *Works*, viii. 3.

as far as possible within into the likeness of a ship : great galleries, and pews, and a fine three-decker, completing the illusion and allowing the saints to sleep comfortably in their beds.

Wesley paid many visits to Whitby and made great friends with a good man there, William Ripley, a steadfast adherent of Methodism : " a burning and a shining light " Wesley called him. He built a chapel between the church steps and the east pier, which very soon fell down, being, as one may see, practically on the sand. It was replaced ere long. In June 1784 Wesley came from Stokesley and Guisborough, and preached in the evening at Whitby.

He says : [1]

*Thurs. and Friday*, 17 *and* 18.—The morning congregation filled the house. Indeed the society here may be a pattern to all in England. They despise all ornaments but good works, together with a meek and quiet spirit. I did not see a ruffle, no, nor a fashionable cap among them ; though many of them are in easy circumstances. I preached at the market-place in the evening, where were at least thrice as many as the house could contain.

19*th*.—I met such a select society as I have not seen since I left London. They were about forty, of whom I did not find one who had not a clear

witness of being saved from inbred sin. Several
of them had lost it for a season, but could never
rest till they had recovered it. And every one of
them seemed now to walk in the full light of God's
countenance.

Again, in 1788, he came and found the
new chapel ready for him, June 12.[1] It still
stands, in Church Street, back from the
road. There is still the pulpit he preached
from, though it has been lowered since his
day ; the table for the Love Feast ; the old
collecting boxes ; the gallery all round ;
truly, to modern taste, a hideous place, but
historically full of interest. It was opened
in 1788, no doubt on the occasion mentioned
in the *Journal* ; and the excitement on the
occasion was intense. The gallery stairs were
not ready and people were let in through the
windows, and then men sat on the edge of
the gallery with their " feet dangled into
space ". This is Wesley's description :

In the evening I preached at Whitby, in the
new house, thoroughly filled above and below ;
though it contains twice as many as the old one ;
and although the unfinished galleries, having as
yet no fronts, were frightful to look upon. It is
the most curious house we have in England. You
go up to it by about forty steps ; and have then
before you a lofty front, I judge near fifty feet
high, and fifty-four feet broad. So much gainers

[1] *Journal*, vii. 400.

have we been by the loss of the former house. Besides that it stood at one end of the town, and in the very sink of it, where people of any fashion were ashamed to be seen.

*Sat.* 14.—At five in the morning we had a large congregation ; but it was more than doubled in the evening ; and at both times I could not but observe the uncommon earnestness of the people.

*Sun.* 15.—The house was well filled at seven. For the sake of the country people, who flocked from all sides, I preached again at half an hour past one on " The end of all things is at hand : be ye therefore sober, and watch unto prayer ". After preaching at five, on the education of children, I made a collection for Kingswood School ; the rather that I might have an opportunity of refuting that poor, threadbare slander of my " getting so much money ". We concluded our service with a comfortable love feast.

The last visit was in June 1790, not far from the end of his life : [1]

*Fri.* 18.—It was very providential that part of the adjoining mountain fell down and demolished our old preaching house, with many houses besides ; by which means we have one of the most beautiful chapels in Great Britain, finely situated on the steep side of the mountain. At six it was pretty well filled with such a congregation of plain, earnest people as is not often seen. I conversed with many of them the next day, who were much alive to God.

*Sun.* 20.—The house contained us at seven tolerably well. The church likewise was well filled. But in the evening we were much strait-ened for room ; but as many as could hear stood on

---

[1] *Journal,* vol. viii. pp. 73-74.

the pavement without. In all England I have not seen a more affectionate people than those at Whitby.

Bristol had one of his last visits ; and again in October 1790 the eastern counties. At Diss in Norfolk he preached in the parish church by the express permission of the wise and generous Bishop Horne, who as Vice-Chancellor at Oxford had condemned the expulsion of six undergraduates from S. Edmund Hall on account of their evangelical doctrine.[1] He returned to London on October 2, 1790. On October 24 he wrote the last notes in his *Journal*, though the brief diary notes continued till within six days of his death. For now the long hard life was near the end.

As we have seen, Samuel Wesley thought his brother John had an " iron constitution " ; but he was constantly ill. So ill had he been in 1753 that he thought he was " far gone in a galloping consumption ". On Monday, September 26, after he had been walking for a long while, in spite of illness, with his usual inexhaustible energy, his doctor ordered him to go into the country and rest, drink asses' milk, and go out riding daily. He wrote an inscription for his own tombstone :

[1] See Canon Ollard's *Six Students*.

Here lieth the body of John Wesley, a brand plucked out of the burning : who died of a consumption in the fifty-first year of his age, not leaving, after his debts are paid, ten pounds behind him : praying God be merciful to me a sinner.

It is very true that he gave away almost all he had in abundant charity, as the *Journal* he published frequently records. " Money never stays with me," he wrote once (October 10, 1746) in his youth ; " it would burn if it did. I throw it out of my hands as soon as possible, lest it should find a way into my heart."

But he was not a good prophet, for instead of dying at fifty he lived to be eighty-eight. And for a long while, as he wrote, his eye was not dimmed nor his natural force abated. But at length he himself felt that he was failing. On January 1, 1790, he had written : [1]

I am now an old man, decayed from head to foot. My eyes are dim ; my right hand shakes much ; my mouth is hot and dry every morning ; I have a lingering fever almost every day : my motion is weak and slow. However, blessed be God, I do not slack my labour. I can preach and write still.

One who was then with him notes that he still rose at four o'clock.

It was now four months from the end.

[1] Vol. viii. p. 35.

For knowledge of this period we are indebted
to an admirable account by Elizabeth Ritchie
(afterwards Mrs. Mortimer), who came to
Wesley's busy house in City Road to help his
old friends Mr. and Mrs. Rogers, who for
some time had had care of him. She read to
him every morning from six o'clock, and
watched over him with most assiduous care.
The record is most touching. The aged man's
indomitable courage, his gentleness, his growing weakness, and his sense of it ; the flashing
up now and then of the flickering life ; the
brief candle of life sinking into the socket : the
tale is very simple. As he became confined
to bed he was constantly heard praying, often
quoting Bible texts and hymns, once or twice
even singing. He died on Tuesday, March 2,
1791. Fully conscious almost to the end, the
last word he said was Farewell. The devoted
friends beside his bed burst into a song of
thanksgiving when all was over.

# CHAPTER VIII

JOHN WESLEY was one of the large army of great little men, like Athanasius, and Chatham, and Nelson, and Wellington, and Lord Roberts. A drawing of him in Edinburgh in 1790 shows him quite small between Dr. Hamilton and Joseph Cole, with whom he is walking arm-in-arm : very neatly dressed, in his long coat, three-cornered hat, knee-breeches, stockings, buckled shoes, a solemn suit of customary black. "A very little fellow" he was, Henry Sacheverell said in 1720, and he hardly grew at all afterwards. His height seems to have not exceeded five feet five inches. In obstinacy and determination of character and readiness to suffer for his opinions he resembled that very tall man, Thomas Becket : in continued confidence in the obvious rightness of his own opinions and actions he resembled that quite short man, Mr. Gladstone.

The portraits of the little great man are extremely numerous, and some of them are very unlike others. No doubt his face was mobile, as are the faces of most orators ; so sometimes it is shown in pathetic solemnity or statuesque calm, sometimes in excited rapture. And the expression seems even to affect the features, to make the nose longer or shorter, the mouth more expansive or more compressed ; but the eyes are always keen and bird-like. The most striking characteristic of every portrait is of course the hair, long, silky, curled at the ends as it flows over the shoulders, obviously the subject of very careful attention. S. Paul thought long hair a shame to a man : Wesley would certainly have said (as perhaps on other matters), " There I disagree with S. Paul ".

There are portraits of Wesley in his two Oxford colleges as well as in the National Portrait Gallery. At Christ Church is a charming, gracious smiling face, attributed to Romney. It is [1] " believed to be one of two contemporary repetitions, differing from it in having the dress trimmed with fur, of the original picture painted December 1788–January 1789, for Mr. Tighe, engraved by J. Spilsbury, 1789, and now in the possession of Mr. Tighe ". Close inspection makes it

[1] *Illustrated Catalogue of Loan Collection*, Oxford, 1906, p. 64 (reproduced as No. 124).

doubtful if there is fur at all, or merely the
black scarf, showing a shadow here and there.
There are two at Lincoln College, one as a
young man, one in old age : neither of the
greatest merit, one somewhat resembling the
Vertue engraving (1745) or possibly that by
Downes. Those at the National Portrait Gallery are : one by Nathaniel Hone, R.A.,
painted when Wesley was sixty-three, showing
dark brown hair, rosy cheeks, and high cheek
bones. The other, the beautiful face of age
—he was eighty-five—with white hair and
face still rosy, is by William Hamilton, R.A.
Of each there is a famous engraving.

Among the many portraits, these two perhaps stand out most prominently. That by
Nathaniel Hone, painted in 1765, has a certain
plumpness, an obvious enthusiasm, perhaps
somewhat of self-satisfaction, but it is quite
clearly a " speaking likeness ". The hand
is raised in encouragement rather than denunciation. The eyes are bright and piercing.
The hair is long and glossy and quite un-
touched by time. Contrast it with the Robert
Hunter, which shows a keener, perhaps a
wiser face, but is not in the least convincing,
or with the rather feeble Zoffany, or the ugly
and aggressive face possibly by George Vertue,
and said to be the first known portrait : then

one sees how differently the mobile features
could appear to different men.   Much pleas-
anter than any of these is that by John Russell,
a most happy, sympathetic face, with the ex-
pressive hands beautifully painted.   In 1789
Romney painted a most beautiful picture—
if one may judge from the engravings :  it is
now in Philadelphia :  it has much the most
charming expression, much the most restful
and natural of all.   Wesley himself evidently
liked it, for he wrote on January 1789, " Mr.
Romney is a painter indeed !  He struck off
an exact likeness at once, and did more in an
hour than Sir Joshua did in ten."   There is
a  charming  " version "  of  this  at  Christ
Church, Oxford.   Some  of the  portraits in
old age are extremely impressive.   There is
one  especially—is  it  by  Barry ?—which, in
a mezzotint, is really extraordinarily beautiful ;  a quite perfect picture of aged sanctity.
Probably no Englishman since Charles I. was
so frequently painted as John Wesley.   Some
of the numerous surviving portraits, as might
be expected, are deplorable.   But from fifty
or  so which can easily be seen one  can  well
summon up a lively likeness of a man so good
and so beloved.[1]   Portraits from time to time

---

[1] There is an excellent book, *Sayings and Portraits of John
Wesley*, by John Telford, Epworth Press, 1924.

emerge from obscurity. In 1926 there has been a controversy about one now at Wesley House, Cambridge, which some suppose to be genuine.

Was John Wesley a learned man ? a question one naturally asks about the leader of an Oxford movement, though the answer hardly matters at all in any estimate of his powers and virtues. A scholar he certainly was, of the eighteenth-century type, with the full qualifications of the Fellow of a College of the period. " The classics " came naturally to his mind for quotation, and to a less degree the principal Fathers of the Church. But also he had read some at least of the Christian Platonists ; knew his Bible very well, with at least a fair appreciation of the Greek and Hebrew ; had enough French, German, and Spanish to read with ease and translate with freedom. Of English literature he was a continuous reader : if his taste was not always what we should consider of the best, he did constantly read and recommend Milton and Shakespeare, George Herbert and Jeremy Taylor, Bunyan and William Law, and a great many of his own contemporaries— the last often rather contemptuously.

The greatest aid to memory is writing, said Bacon ; and Wesley's facility of speech from a well-stored mind was largely due, no doubt, to his custom as a young man of analysing and making extracts from the books he read. He said of himself that he " collected ". The expression has been oddly explained by the painstaking editor of the *Journal* [1] with a reference to what he calls " collection ", and explains, from the *Century Dictionary*, as " a private examination at the end of each term at the colleges of the English Universities ". There is of course no privacy about the matter, and the word " collections " is always used in the plural. " A consectary " (that is a corollary), says Dr. Johnson : and Wesley no doubt meant that he put his reading together into a form from which he could draw conclusions. His reading was miscellaneous. It is interesting to discover that he read not only classics and theology, but that he wasted his time (as his modern editor thinks) over Ben Jonson and tales of pirates. Perhaps he read too widely ; but can one read too widely ? Let us take a passage or two from the *Journal*. Thus he wrote of Chesterfield and of Fénelon : [2]

I borrowed here a volume of Lord Chesterfield's *Letters*, which I had heard very strongly commended.

[1] Nehemiah Curnock in the " Standard edition " of the *Journal*, i. 20 *note*.
[2] Vol. vi. p. 80, October 1775.

And what did I learn ? That he was a man of much wit, middling sense, and some learning, but as absolutely void of virtue as any Jew, Turk or heathen that ever lived. I say, not only void of all religion (for I doubt whether he believed there is a God, though he tags most of his letters with the name, for better sound sake) but even of virtue, of justice, and mercy, which he never once recommended to his son. And truth he sets at open defiance : he continually guards him against it. Half his letters inculcate deep dissimulation as the most necessary of all accomplishments. Add to this his studiously instilling into the young man all the principles of debauchery, when himself was between seventy and eighty years old. Add his cruel censure of that amiable man the Archbishop of Cambray (*quantum dispar illi*) as a mere time-serving hypocrite ! And this is the favourite of the age ! Whereas, if justice and truth take place, if he is rewarded according to his desert, his name will stink to all generations.

The extent of his reading is thus illustrated by Mr. Abbey : [1]

We find, for instance, during the years 1768–73, that he had read during that time, among other works, Leland's *History of Ireland*, Bonavicini's *History of the War in Italy*, Wodrow on the *Persecution in Scotland*, Dalrymple's *Memoirs of the Revolution*, Walpole's *Critical Notes on the Times of Richard III.*, much of Mosheim's *Ecclesiastical History*, Hooke's *Roman History*, *Belisarius*, *Life of Pope Sixtus V.*, *An Account of the European Settlements in America*, a great part of Homer's

---

[1] *The English Church and its Bishops, 1700–1800*, vol. i. pp. 263-264 *note*.

**M**

*Odyssey*, Thomson's *Poems*, Dr. Byrom's *Poems*, Blackburne on the *Penal Laws*, *Medical Essays*, Priestley on *Electricity*, the pleadings in the Douglas Case, several of Swedenborg's writings, etc. On most of these he makes in his diary a few short and pithy remarks.

It would not be a very bad list for a country parson, apart from his ordinary theological reading ; even at the present enlightened day there may be some rural clergy who do not read so much ; but Wesley, we must remember, was hardly ever at leisure. Had he any home at all ? Certainly he had no quiet country rectory ; and he had taken the world for his parish. In his case, as in that of the clergyman of to-day with whom we compare him, we make no mention of newspapers. Mark Pattison once said that he never polluted his mind with them until after five o'clock in the afternoon. There were far fewer of them in Wesley's day to distract the intelligence of man ; but there is no doubt at all that what there were, were not neglected by the great evangelist. He probably regarded a knowledge of current events, and of fugitive and ill-informed judgements on them, as a necessary part of the education and equipment of a preacher. So do many modern clergymen : with what results who shall say ?

It is generally supposed that the reading of newspapers produces a slippery or slip-shod manner of writing, and those who preach in a hurry as well as write in haste naturally fall into this fault. Wesley was certainly aware of the danger. Thus he wrote :

Tues. 8 [June 1790].  I wrote a form for settling the preaching houses, without any superfluous words, which shall be used for the time to come, verbatim, for all the houses to which I contribute anything. I will no more encourage that villainous tautology of lawyers, which is the scandal of our nation.

But the objection here is not so much to a matter of ordinary English good writing as to the peculiarities of a class towards whom he, like many other preachers, bore no good-will.  If you cannot find fault with a lawyer's judgement, you can, so the preacher thinks, with his language : he is too precise, or too technical, too crabbed or too diffuse.  Do extremes really meet ?  Can a lawyer and a journalist have the same faults ?  Lawyers' English, surely, is regulated and precise : journalists' is the reverse.

Wesley had certainly, according to a more modern standard, no sense of " style ".  He accuses the lawyers of tautology.  He was diffuse himself.  " More matter with less art," a critic might say to him.  He would certainly reply, " Madam, I swear I use no art at all." But that would not be true. Horace Walpole was not wholly wrong when he said that the great preacher was an actor. And an actor has much affinity with a newspaper man.

But Wesley did not need a study of the newspapers to teach him fluidity : it belonged to his very nature. " Silly Billy ", who meant " voluminous " when he was asked why he had praised Gibbon so highly in calling him " luminous ", might have better applied the adjective to John Wesley. The great Gibbon was not an exceptionally prolific writer, but Wesley's output was stupendous. At least four hundred publications are authentically credited to his pen. He was not only a considerable writer himself, but he was a practised and unblushing book-maker. He was in fact a pioneer in popular education, the precursor of Lord Brougham and the pedants whom Thomas Love Peacock derided. He had the audacity to abridge Bunyan and Milton and George Herbert ; he regarded anybody else's text as the legitimate field for his improving genius. He set to work to drive out the old chap-books by his new tracts, which, as he says, were generally sold at a penny apiece.

Wesley was certainly the most audacious of editors. To improve the works of the illustrious dead was a common form of literary enterprise in the early eighteenth century, and beyond. So Dryden improved Chaucer, and Shakespeare was improved by David Garrick and Nahum Tate. Wesley took upon himself to treat a living author in the same way. In 1780 he published Henry Brooke's *Fool of Quality* in a revised edition. He had found the tale too " whimsical " for his taste, and he used the scissors on its five volumes trenchantly. The result is an extraordinary combination of Richardson, Fielding, Smollett, Lillo, and Methodist theology ; it is crowded with murders and rapes, overloaded with incident and excitement, as full of immoral scenes as of pious expressions, of fisticuffs as (in the language of a later day) of sobstuff : and Wesley recommended it (in his own version) as " the most excellent in its kind of any that I have seen, either in English or any other language ". After reading this, and what he says of it, one is tempted to wonder whether Wesley had any literary conscience or any literary taste. In the original the crowd of exciting incident is interspersed with philosophic dialogue and reflection. Both are tedious, but when they are so near together they modify each other. But Wesley was impatient of the reflection and extracted a moral meaning from the incident : he suppressed a great part of the one and thus exaggerated the other : he removed the balance, which indeed had a certain literary art in it ; and the result is to make the book, as he presented it, tedious to the very limit of the unbearable. The fact is that, in regard to literature as in life, Wesley presents a persistent paradox. He could himself write extremely well, and he knew what good writing was ; and yet sometimes as a judge of literature he seemed to know no more than an idiot or a child of fourteen.

What survives of all this mass ? Some things murkily among obscure readers. Some New Testament suggestions as anticipatory of later students. (It is curious that he applies the same words to Bengel that Laud used of Andrewes : *lumen orbis Christiani*.) A few sermons, belated survivors from the devouring flood which has drowned the pulpit eloquence of the eighteenth century.

But the *Journal* certainly, for all its immense length, is immortal ; side by side in date it stands with Walpole's Letters, in form not dissimilar, but in content and spirit how widely different. It possesses two remarkable merits.  First, it is an absolutely truthful revelation of the man, in his devotion, sincerity, hardihood, self - confidence, and vanity.  And secondly, it is written in a style which is almost like John Henry Newman's in its approach to the perfection of limpid and beautiful English.  He wrote once : " What constitutes a good style ?  Perspicuity, purity, propriety, strength, and easiness joined together " ;  and there could be no better description of what constitutes the excellence of his own writing.  He can be gentle and soothing ;  he can be savage and biting ;  he can be laborious and meticulous ;  but hardly ever does he fail to be perfectly direct, plain, emphatic, and vigorous.  The force of his writing is due to the fact that it was always natural.  When one reads what he has written it is very difficult to believe that he ever blotted a line.  And yet he is hardly ever verbose.  Mr. Chadband does not trace his literary ancestry from John Wesley, but from John Wesley's untrained and illiterate successors.  Always natural : and the true test of that is a man's letters.  Letters written for effect are abominable things, and almost always betray themselves.  No such charge can be brought against John Wesley.

There is a real interest attaching to re-

ligious letters or (what is by no means always
the same thing) letters of religious men. No
doubt there are among them some hypocritical effusions, stagey, dressed-up produc-
tions as deficient in sincerity or as obviously
the product of laborious artifice as election
addresses or the semi-private letters to con-
stituents which politicians used to find so
useful, or at least redolent of the hypocrisy
analysed by Bishop Butler in his famous
sermon on King Charles's Day. But much
more often they have a genuine sincerity
which belongs at once to the theme and to
the writer, and they gain rather than lose by
the absence of those trivialities from which
the ordinary letter derives much of its charm.
It would not be an affectation to prefer the
letters of Fénelon to those of Mme. de
Sévigné, though such a choice may not be
common. The letters of Cowper stand mid-
way between the two, and they will never
lose their place among precious things. Nor
do modern times engross the interest among
such epistles. It is not easy to match the
grave wisdom of S. Gregory, the power and
splendour of S. Bernard, the vehement
vigour of S. Thomas of Canterbury. Luther
has left a few letters that belong to the
treasures of man's history. The matchless

epistles of Erasmus can hardly be placed in the same category, yet to those who know them they are of more enduring worth. Like all letters, the religious epistles of the Reformers taste best when they are most simple and most personal. And that character lasts down to our own time and gives fascination to nearly all Newman's letters, to some of Pusey's and Keble's and Kingsley's, and to very many in those remarkable volumes which contain too few of the vast number written by Richard Meux Benson. On the other side, it must be admitted, we have the two bulky volumes of Mr. Gladstone's *Religious Letters*, which, it may safely be said, will not survive, in spite of their admirable editing, and will be remembered only for a few scattered gems in them, like that in which the writer describes his introduction, during a day's grouse-shooting, to the pleasures of " partridge-eyed champagne ".

It would not be difficult to assert for the letters of John Wesley a high place in the long list. He had nearly all the qualities of a perfect letter-writer. He wrote clearly, simply, quickly, pungently, with transparent sincerity, and he hardly ever used two words where one would do. His letters, indeed, are the letters of an honest man who conceals nothing, sets down naught in malice, but much in candour, and has for supreme interest nothing but goodness and those who do good.[1]  Indeed, it is their vivacity which makes Wesley's letters immortal.  One side of Wesley's letter writing has long won a certain notoriety.  It belongs to that " predilection for the female character " of which Southey spoke so gently.  It is impossible not to regret, when one remembers the essay on John Knox, that R. L. Stevenson did not try his hand at this amusing aspect of Wesley's career ; equally impossible, when one recalls the essay on Burns, not to rejoice that it did not attract the attention of W. E. Henley.[2]

Wesley's letters, indeed, cover, as does his *Journal*, every side of his extraordinarily manifold activity.  If he does not often turn to Shakespeare, taste, and the musical glasses, he does not ignore, though he may reprobate, the side of life to which they belong.  But

[1] In *Letters of John Wesley* Mr. Eayrs has done a most praiseworthy thing in making a selection of them ; it is a large one, not a little of it is comparatively new, and while very few pages lack serious value a great many contain delightful passages of humour and vivacity.

[2] The best thing that has been written on the subject is the charming book of M. Leger, of Brest, on *John Wesley's Last Love*, but Mr. Eayrs has given us some good letters and not unreasonable comments.  It is easy to see, though no one doubts for a moment Wesley's essential goodness, that he laid himself open, in his effusive sincerity of affection, to unkind criticism, which, side by side with his autocracy, had some share in consequences of far-reaching importance.

it is natural for him to be critical, for he was profoundly opinionative.

The particular controversies in which he was so continually engaged are for the most part exceedingly dusty now, but his own expressions about them are as fresh as ever. Most of all this is true when he deals with persons. He had a direct way of telling people their faults, and setting them right, which must have been extraordinarily unpleasing to the subjects of his wit or wisdom, but is extremely refreshing to ourselves. He had six hundred and ninety itinerant preachers under him. He ruled them like a regiment. He did not care in the least whether they were learned men, as some of them were, or clever, as were many. He wrote to them in the same commanding tone, very often kindly, always piously, never without a sincerity which they must have been less or more than human if they did not sometimes resent. It certainly cannot truthfully be asserted that these men were " all of rare devotion " ; some of them were certainly extremely conceited, perhaps self-seeking, young persons. The excellent Mr. Richard Graves in his *Spiritual Quixote* drew directly from life. Wesley knew well enough the kind of man with whom he had often to deal. If he advised them and they

" took it as an affront " he repeated the
advice. Here is a letter of 1775 to John King : [1]

Scream no more, at the peril of your soul. God
now warns you by me, whom He has set over you.
Speak as earnestly as you can, but do not scream.
Speak with all your heart, but with a moderate
voice. It was said of Our Lord, " He shall not
cry " ; the word properly means, He shall not
scream. Herein be a follower of me, as I am of
Christ.

He endorsed this good advice by the
example of two good men who were " in
grievous darkness before they died ", and
assured his correspondent that he was
" stubborn and headstrong ".

John Wesley was quite as candid a critic
in literature as in morals. He told his
brother Charles that some of his hymns were
" namby - pambical ". He explained very
clearly to several correspondents what was
the essence of style. He warned against
stiffness ; he found " all the proprieties of
a good writer " in South, Atterbury, and
Swift. He quoted Pope, in the famous lines
which begin with

Poets themselves must die, like those they sung,

and said " This crowns all ; no stiffness, no
hard words ; no apparent act, no affectation ;

[1] *John Wesley's Letters* (Eayrs), p. 253.

all is natural, and therefore consummately beautiful. Go thou and write likewise." The young gentleman to whom he wrote thus was not at all pleased ; it is the way of such. He argued ; and so Wesley wrote again : " I wanted to have you write in the most excellent way : if you prefer any other, you may ". He was quite as sensible when he advised people about their health as when he tried to correct their style. He told the Conference why so many preachers fell into " nervous disorders ", and specialists to-day say no more than he did and prescribe no differently. Indeed, Mr. Eayrs's collection shows him advising on every subject under the sun, and, it must be admitted, whether he was competent or not, advising, too, always as an autocrat. He told the exasperating Wride that the Conference, "while I live, is the preachers whom I *invite* to confer with me ", and reminded him that when the stewards once claimed to be " the people's ", not his, he simply dismissed them and named others in their place.

There can be little doubt, nor any reason why it should not be admitted now that most people can afford to look at the matter historically, that it was this autocratic spirit more than anything else which caused the

separation. Mr. Eayrs, in his valuable collection of the letters, to which I have so
frequently referred, does not quote any of
the strongest statements of Wesley's attachment to the Church or denunciation of those
who would leave it ; but he does give the
letter to James Knox which says that, far
from leaving the Church, if he followed his
advice he would do just the contrary, but
lose no opportunity of attending her services
and steadily adhere to her doctrine ; just as
he told his brother Charles that the practical
conclusion—" did we not all agree in that ? "
—was " not to separate from the Church " ;
and John Nelson, that rather than see him
a dissenting minister " I wish to see thee
smiling in thy coffin ". For all Charles
Wesley's epigram about the ease of laying
hands " by man or woman's whim ", it was
Wesley's temper, not his theology, in which
lay the seeds of separation.

This temper, so self-confident as well as
so straightforward, gives a special force to his
letters to public men, such as those to
George III., to North, and to Pitt, several
to civic officers, the famous one in which
he told the Excise man that he had four
silver teaspoons and did not intend to buy
any more in war time, and that other—

which reminds us how often his advice is as good to-day as when he wrote it—wherein he complained (during the Rebellion of 1745) of the ignorant profaneness of the poor men to whom our lives are entrusted, and the " continual cursing, and swearing, the wanton blasphemy, of the soldiers in general ".

Wesley, in fact, was certainly a great letter writer, though as certainly he was not a great " man of letters ". Of other sides of his literary activity something has already been said. He was a fluent pamphleteer and a sober sermon writer. As a poet an admirer has been moved to think that his " contributions to Methodist psalmody may yet prove at least as lasting as those of his brother ", and has spoken of his " chaste and stately verse ".[1] The prophecy seems unlikely of fulfilment, and the eulogy is almost absurd. John Wesley was certainly not a poet. The hymns of Charles, on the other hand, contain some of the finest religious verse in the English language. John Wesley's fame rests on a firmer basis.

The effects of his great religious work were twofold. He revived the passion of English priests for the poor. This had never wholly passed away. There is indeed

[1] *A New History of Methodism*, vol. i. p. 251.

no period of English history—the days of
S. Cuthbert and Bede, of the Friars, of
George Herbert, of Joseph Butler travelling
over the great area of his Weardale parish on
a shaggy pony—in which there have not been
English clergy to deserve the eulogy of
Chaucer. But certainly a new life was put
into their work by the fervour of Wesley.
Once again the English Church made a
gigantic effort to become the Church of the
people. This effort no doubt was primarily
concerned with the conversion of the individual, and kept rather in the background
the thought of the solidarity of the Church,
the succession of its teachers, the inheritance
of its faith. The continuous inspiration of
the Holy Spirit in the Body of Christ tended
to become a truth neglected for the equally
essential truth of the access of the individual
to God. But no one can say that the idea
of a Christian Society was ever forgotten by
Wesley or the Methodists. The smaller
bodies were linked together in bonds of
Christian love, if the larger whole and its
history were sometimes forgotten. But the
indirect influence of Wesley was almost as
great outside as within the sphere of pure
religion. At a time when all Europe was
disturbed, when politics seemed to be the

realisation of a volcano, the fact that men's thoughts in England were turned to the things of God and the soul preserved the country from any share in the foreign revolution. It was Wesley's influence which made men feel that the things of the soul were paramount, and social and political conditions only secondary. There were bad results of this, as seen in the worst side of the industrial revolution. But no one who compares England during the revolutionary period, not with France only, but with Germany, Italy, or Spain, can fail to see that the conditions of life in England were far happier than those in other parts of Europe. And more than anything else the cause of this was the work of Wesley. The appeal to men's consciences touched the rich as well as the poor. Country squires, London merchants, as well as tradespeople, were taught to rule their lives by the divine law. Inadequately and unequally indeed was this done. But done it was, over a wide area; and English life became more honest, more philanthropic, and more pure. Many a great movement of amelioration and emancipation won strength from the influence, widely disseminated, of John Wesley. There were sayings of his which went straight to men's

N

hearts. " We are called to propagate Bible religion through the land ; that is, faith working by love ; holy tempers and holy lives." Thoughts such as these do indeed bring forth in men the fruit of good living. " I have thought, I am a creature of a day, passing through life as an arrow through the air. I am a spirit come from God and returning to God "—there could not be a better motto for John Wesley's life.

Methodism awoke a new spirit in the Church of England. It did not create, but it reinvigorated that section of it which began to be called, peculiarly, Evangelical. As Wesley's last letter shows, it gave a new force to philanthropic effort, which the religious societies had fostered centuries before. Indirectly it influenced many who were outside the direct influence of either Methodist or Evangelical. There is much that suggests their mental and spiritual attitude in Wordsworth, something in Coleridge, something even in Southey, the admiring yet severe critic of Wesley and his followers. The influence of Wesley indeed, even within the Church of England, radiates far and wide to-day. And the works of the separated body which he so unwillingly founded are known and read of all men.

# INDEX

*Printed in Great Britain by* R. & R. CLARK, LIMITED, *Edinburgh.*

# GREAT ENGLISH CHURCHMEN SERIES

EDITED BY

## SIDNEY DARK

Crown 8vo.

THOMAS ARNOLD. By Rev. R. J. Campbell, D.D.

ST. THOMAS OF CANTERBURY. By Sidney Dark.

THOMAS CRANMER. By Rev. Anthony C. Deane, Hon. Canon of Worcester Cathedral.

ARCHBISHOP LAUD. By A. S. Duncan-Jones.

JOHN WESLEY. By the Very Rev. W. H. Hutton, D.D., Dean of Winchester.

*Other volumes to follow.*

MACMILLAN & CO., LTD., LONDON

# NEW THEOLOGICAL WORKS

REALITY. A New Correlation of Science and
Religion. By Burnett Hillman Streeter,
Canon of Hereford. 8vo. 8s. 6d. net.

"A brilliant survey of the field of thought as it appears to-day ;
more than that, it is a brilliant strategic occupation of it in the
interests of a spiritual philosophy."—*The Times Literary Supplement*.

THE SYNOPTIC GOSPELS. Edited, with an
Introduction and a Commentary, by C. G.
Montefiore. *Second Edition.* 2 vols. 8vo.

An attempt to discuss and appraise the teaching contained in
the first three gospels from a liberal Jewish point of view, and at
the same time to give a clear statement of the various critical
problems involved, and concise explanations of the words of the
gospels with an English translation based upon that of the A.V.

VISIONS OF THE SPIRITUAL WORLD.
A Brief Description of the Spiritual Life, its
Different States of Existence, and the
Destiny of Good and Evil Men as seen in
Visions. By Sadhu Sundar Singh. Crown
8vo. 2s. 6d. net.

"A large public will gladly welcome 'Visions of the Spiritual
World.'"—*The Church of England Newspaper*.

HANDBOOK TO THE TEXTUAL CRITI-
CISM OF THE NEW TESTAMENT.
By Sir Frederic G. Kenyon, K.C.B., F.B.A.
*Second Edition. New Impression.* With 16
Facsimiles. Extra crown 8vo. 8s. 6d. net.

"The best introduction to its subject which a student can
find."—*The British Weekly*.

MACMILLAN & CO., LTD., LONDON